THE
RIVER LAVANT

The River Lavant, Chichester.

THE
RIVER LAVANT

CHICHESTER'S RIVER FROM SOURCE TO MOUTH

KEN NEWBURY

Phillimore

First published 1987
Reprinted 1994

Second edition, 2000
Published by
PHILLIMORE & CO. LTD.
Shopwyke Manor Barn, Chichester, West Sussex

ISBN 1 86077 162 9

.

Printed in Great Britain by
ST RICHARDS PRESS
Chichester, West Sussex

Contents

List of Illustrations vii

Illustration Acknowledgements viii

Foreword ix

Introduction xi

1. Derivations: A Lavant Poem 1
2. Origins 3
3. East Dean to West Dean 4
4. On to East Lavant 9
5. Fordwater and Graylingwell 12
6. Westhampnett 15
7. Nearing Chichester 19
8. St Pancras: Flooding 21
9. To Kingsham and Round the Walls 27
10. Under the City 31
11. Beating the Bounds 34
12. Whose Responsibility? 36
13. A Carrier of Disease 39
14. A Clean Bill of Health at Last 43
15. On to Appledram 47
16. 'Rippling Waves ...' 52
17. The Floods of January 1994 53
18. The Floods of November 2000 63

Source Material 65

Index 67

List of Illustrations

Frontispiece: The River Lavant, Chichester

1.	Map showing the course of the river Lavant	xii
2.	Behind Singleton	2
3.	The Lavant at Charlton	5
4.	Singleton Pond	6
5.	Sluice gate at Singleton	6
6.	The Lavant at West Dean Gardens	7
7.	Sheepwash Lane at Lavant	10
8.	Below East Lavant road bridge	12
9.	The ford at Fordwater	13
10.	The Grayling Well	14
11.	Westhampnett Mill	16
12.	Sluice for Westhampnett Mill	16
13.	Plan: Westhampnett Mill, *c.*1921	17
14.	St James's Hospital	21
15.	The Lavant at Riverside, St Pancras	23
16.	Floods at New Park Road, pre-1887	25
17.	John Norden's map of Chichester, 1595	28
18.	Section of culvert under Eastgate Square	29
19.	The garden of 'Market Walls', in Market Avenue	29
20.	Culverting under Market Road	30
21.	William Gardner's map of Chichester, 1769	32
22.	The footpath from Fishbourne to Dell Quay	38
23.	Typhoid Map, 1879	42
24.	Westgate Fields	46
25.	The Lavant, the College of Further Education	46
26.	Map of the Lavant at Westgate, 1846	48
27.	The Lavant near Appledram Lane	49
28.	Plan: Diversion at Harbour sluice, 1945	50
29.	The Last of the Lavant	52
30.	Floodwater at Westhampnett	53
31.	Chichester by-pass between Whyke and Bognor roundabouts	54
32.	The flooded A27 east of Chichester	54
33.	The A27 and Maudlin Farm from the air	55
34.	Bailey bridge on the A259 at Merston	56
35.	Bailey bridge and pontoon at Westhampnett roundabout	57
36.	Sandbags at the Castle Market, Chichester	58
37.	West Sussex Fire Brigade's sandbags	58

38. The River Lavant in full flow through Chichester 59
39. The Hornet, looking towards Eastgate Square 60
40. Floodwater in the Hornet, looking west.. 60
41. Floodwater in the Hornet, looking east 61
42. Preparations in East Street, Chichester 62
43. Milk float in Yapton 62
44. Rising water in Delling Lane, Bosham 63
45. Flooding: St Pancras, Chichester 63
46. New Park Road, Chichester 64
47. Flood relief piping at Old Market Avenue, Chichester 64

Illustration Acknowledgements

Illustrations nos. 1-29 are from the author's collection; nos. 30, 33-36, 39-41 and 43
are reproduced by kind permission of George Godden; nos. 32 and 44-47 by kind
permission of Portsmouth Publishing and Printing Ltd., and nos. 31, 37, 38 and 42
by kind permission of Tony Morris.

The author and publisher are most grateful for assistance with photographs
from January 1994 and November 2000 to John Williams and Tony Morris of the
Emergency Planning Office; to George Godden; and to Peter Homer of the *Chichester
Observer*.

Foreword to the First Edition

By Geoffrey Godber, C.B.E., D.L.

Living, as I do, within a few yards of the Lavant in its upper reaches, I am delighted to be able to commend this book. Not only does it explore the lovely countryside of the Lavant valley but, with the aid of a wealth of careful research, it unfolds the social history of all that is interwoven with it.

It was the dramatic change that took place thousands of years ago in the geological structure of southern England, when the swampy lake where dinosaurs fed suffered the great eruptions which thrust up the downs and drained the Wealden lake, which gave birth to the Lavant, and Mr. Newbury tells us how this most modest of rivers has fared since then and how it has served the needs of man.

A knowledge of the geological, geographical and social background of our local scene cannot but improve our enjoyment of it. The Lavant as it is today drains the area south of Duncton and Cocking hills and each year, when enough rain has fallen to fill the spongy chalk of the uplands and saturate the valley gravels, the springs burst forth and the Lavant comes into its own again—yet always it is flowing unseen in the gravel below, even when its course is drained on the surface. In Singleton, we can always find water a few feet below ground level, except in drought years.

I fancy that what will surprise readers most is the revelation of how the City fathers turned a blind eye on the pollution and infection that resulted from their failure to enforce proper standards of hygiene and to provide for drainage long after the lessons had been learned in the bigger towns. It is as a social record as well as in the capture of the country scene that this book will make a lasting appeal.

Introduction

It is perhaps not surprising that comparatively few people I have talked to are able to describe the course of the River Lavant for the whole of its length from source to mouth. The adjective most frequently applied to our little stream is intermittent—a term which is equally appropriate to its seasonal appearances and disappearances and to the number of times it goes out of sight in its brief journey to the sea. Although delighting in the fact that Chichester possessed a river, however small and elusive, I realised that my own knowledge of its extent and history was equally limited when one day I responded to an invitation to give a talk on the subject, which involved me in many happy hours of exploration and research. The overwhelming response to the several lectures I have since given persuaded me that there is room among our local history publications for some more permanent record of our Lavant river.

The information contained here is based on personal observation, on research in the County Record Office and the Local Studies section in Chichester Public Library, on conversations with local residents, and on letters, often from complete strangers. These responses and the enthusiasm with which my enquiries were met have been among the most rewarding experiences arising from my studies. I am indeed grateful to all those people who have helped me in this work. I hope they will understand if I do not name them all here, but record my special thanks to Ken Green for his work on the maps and diagrams; to Noel Osborne of Phillimore for editorial guidance; and to Geoffrey Godber for contributing the Foreword.

The appearance of a new edition of my little book naturally gives me much pleasure. Ever since the 1994 floods people have been asking—'Is there going to be a follow-up?'. Unfortunately failing eyesight and other considerations have made this impossible.

The disastrous floods naturally awake far greater interest in the River Lavant, but I believe that local people will always wish to learn about their river, in peaceful as well as calamitous periods of its existence.

K.N.

November 2000

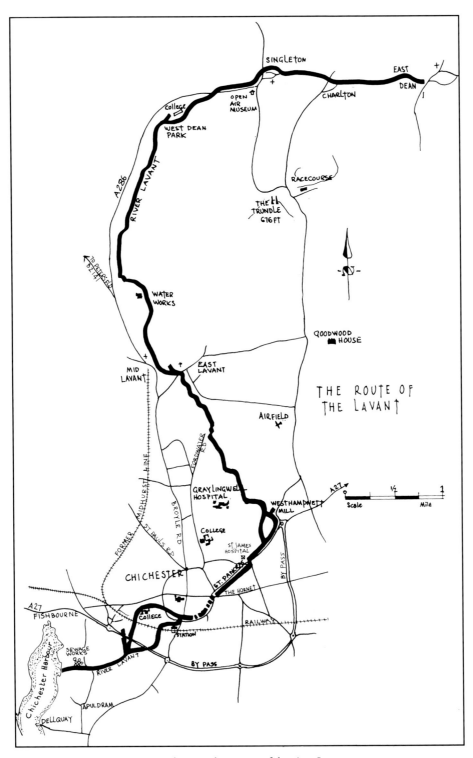

1 Map showing the course of the river Lavant.

Chapter One

Derivations: A Lavant Poem

A S WE SHALL SEE, the Lavant has suffered many changes in the course of its short journey. In fact, in the report of the Sussex River Authority for the year ending March 1969, under Chichester Division, it is stated that 'there is now no section of main river left in a natural state'. Briefly its present-day route is as follows: it appears first in the valley running westward from East Dean to Singleton, thence to West Dean where it turns south to run between Mid and East Lavant and on through fields via Fordwater bridge. On reaching Westhampnett Road it turns sharply south-west, passing along and under various roads and buildings in Chichester to emerge at Westgate Fields, finally reaching Chichester Harbour at a point between Fishbourne and Appledram. Later chapters describe in more detail its adventures along the way.

According to Eilert Ekwall's authoritative work, *The Concise Oxford Dictionary of English Place-names* (1980), the name LAVANT is derived from the Latin 'labor', to glide, slide or trickle, and is identical in origin with the LOVAT both in Buckinghamshire and in Scotland, and with the LAVANT in the Austrian province of Carinthia. Variations in spelling were common in the past: Loventone in Domesday Book, Louentona, Lavent, Lovente. The word in southern dialect signifies a land-spring breaking out in the downs, a brook that is dry in some seasons—certainly applicable to our stream. W.D. Parish's *Dictionary of the Sussex Dialect* (1981) gives alternative derivations, though Ekwall is to be preferred: from 'lafian', Anglo-Saxon, to sprinkle with water; or the French 'laver', to wash. It gives the definition 'A violent flow of water', and quotes as an example of its use in Sussex dialect: 'How it did rain! It ran down the street in a lavant!'

To describe the present-day Lavant as a violent flow of water may seem an exaggeration, but it has not always been such a placid stream. It has claimed several lives over the years, and has often been the cause of serious flooding and other disasters. One poet, at any rate, was in no doubt as to its potency, as the following lines show:

> I've seen thy waters with a torrent's force
> Restless and with loud and rushing sound
> Dash forward in their wild impetuous course,
> As if they scorned thy channel's narrow bound;
> While Winter on the naked landscape frowned
> In sullen majesty, and with a blast terrific,
> Call'd his gathering storms around:
> Black Ruin followed quite, where'er they passed
> And o'er creation's force thick gloom and horror cast.

2   Behind Singleton.

These lines are from a poem, *The Lavant*, a work of 17 verses by one of Chichester's minor poets, Charles Crocker. Whilst his verses are contemplative rather than descriptive, I feel that tribute should be paid here to a local writer who held the river in such affection.

Crocker was born in the city of poor parents in June 1797. He had a limited education locally till, at the age of seven, and through the influence of friends, he was able to attend the Greycoat School for the next four years. Always fond of books, he read all he could. When he was twelve, he was apprenticed to a shoemaker; seven years later he became a journeyman in that trade, but while his hands were busy his thoughts were full of poetry. As he says in the poem, '... My mind e'en while my hands stern Labour's shackles wear, in Poesy a solace sweet shall find.' Through his verse he became a friend of Robert Southey, who admired his writings to such an extent that he considered Crocker's sonnet 'To the British Oak' one of the finest in the English language. Certainly his first published volume of poems brought in a large profit. He married, but his wife died only two years later, leaving him to bring up an infant daughter. He later remarried. In 1839 he left his former trade to go into a more appropriate calling, as bookseller for Mr. Hayley Mason, a local printer and publisher. Six years later he became sexton at Chichester Cathedral. His services were so satisfactory that he was subsequently appointed Bishop's Verger. He became something of an authority on the architecture of the building, and wrote a guide, A *Visit to Chichester Cathedral*. His collected poems were published in 1859. Crocker was devoted to the Cathedral. It was believed that he was so shocked by the fall of the spire in February 1861 that it hastened his death in the following October. He left two daughters and a son.

However tame and well-behaved the flow of water may be today, at the time of the Domesday survey there was sufficient force to power four mills, two in the Singleton-Lavant area, one at Westhampnett and one in Chichester, of which more will be told later.

Chapter Two

Origins

THE LAVANT AS WE KNOW IT TODAY is a very different affair from the watercourse which created it. Now a mere nine miles in length, it was at one time larger than the river Rother and, if nature had acted differently, might have been as important a river in Sussex as the Arun or the Adur. To the layman, the fact that its origins lie somewhere to the north of present-day Midhurst is difficult to accept, bearing in mind the existence of the line of the South Downs that now runs between that town and the coast. More learned authorities have suggested the following explanation.

The possible primary 'trunk' route for the Lavant could have been initiated about ten million years ago. This original route would have extended considerably northwards of the present line of the chalk escarpment of the South Downs. At that time in the geological past, the scarp itself would have been further north, thus giving a considerably larger drainage area. There is strong circumstantial evidence that the scarp *has* retreated southwards due to the effect of weathering and erosion. This larger area could account for the firm establishment of the Lavant and its subsequent, albeit modified, survival. With the backwearing of the scarp, rocks beneath the chalk became exposed at the surface along roughly east-west belts. Weaker rocks in this series allowed the river Rother to develop, as a tributary of the Arun, by cutting headwards (back) from east to west. Because of the relative lack of erosional resistance in the sandstone through which it runs, the Rother has developed more vigorously than its older neighbour, the Lavant, with its chalk substratum. This gradual working back of the Rother resulted in the headwaters of the Lavant being 'captured'.

The marked bend in the Lavant at West Dean is very significant. The upper course of the present stream (i.e. Charlton-Singleton) lies within an eroded fold, or anticline; the probability is that an original tributary of the Lavant eroded back in an easterly direction, in its turn capturing, or beheading, minor streams that originally made their way southwards. Over the centuries, there have been many more changes in the course of the river, most of them man-made.

Chapter Three

East Dean to West Dean

ANYONE HOPING TO FIND THE PRECISE BIRTHPLACE OF THE LAVANT will be disappointed. It first makes its appearance in or close to the village of East Dean, where the water bubbles up in the form of springs in the roadway and gardens. In the 1950s and 1960s it appeared in the cellars of the local inn, *The Star and Garter,* but steps have more recently been taken to prevent this. The timing of its first showing and of its duration is equally unpredictable; February seems the preferred month, but in 1956 it showed itself in November, when the green was flooded from side to side, the roads were under water, and the Rural District Council had to put a temporary gangway from the chapel to the bus stop. (This would no longer be necessary as the bus service was discontinued several years ago.) There were floods again in the following year, when the river rose about half a mile eastward above the village, ruining the winter wheat in the Bury field.

I am asked what causes the sporadic nature of the Lavant. As the Portsmouth Water Company put it succinctly in reply to my enquiry: 'The flow in the Lavant only occurs when the water rises above ground level'. The amount of water underground depends partly on the rainfall of the previous season. My belief is that with the increasing number of houses built within its catchment area the rain that would previously have drained into the land is now channelled directly into the drains and is lost to the Lavant. As we know, once the river is in spate, it continues for some months; February to June or July is a fair average, but in some periods it has survived for much longer. For instance, it flowed continuously from 5 January 1958 to 18 August 1959.

To return to East Dean: in recent years, the tendency has been for water first to appear in the ditch on the north side of the road between that village and Charlton, as it did in March 1985 when I first began to take a closer interest in the river. Water can still be found in East Dean pond from time to time, but in the 1920s it was a source of supply for the filling of field troughs and for road spraying.

Before reaching Charlton the Lavant, now a trickle, crosses under the road to the south side. Almost opposite this point *is The Fox Goes Free* pub. A board in one of the bars commemorates an event of national significance. In its earlier existence as a simple, presumably tied *Fox,* the first Women's Institute meeting in England was held in that room on 9 November 1915. The stream continues more or less in company with the road almost to Singleton, back under the road again through a rough area on the edge of a neglected burial ground west of the village school, reappearing to flow under the road bridge, into Singleton pond. Ian Serraillier, in his book *All Change at Singleton,* has two photographs of this pond. He mentions a notice prohibiting the draining of water there for traction engines, though this could be done opposite *The Horse and Groom,* but carts, waggons and timber drays from Charlton sawmill regularly splashed through. This prevented the wooden wheels from shrinking and allowing the iron tyres to work loose. No doubt too it was a welcome opportunity for refreshment for the horses.

The stream now passes under the A286 to emerge on the west side of the road, then behind gardens to reappear in front of the Post Office and follow the edge of the village cricket field.

As we have seen earlier, the section from East Dean was in geological times merely a tributary of the true river, and signs of this still exist, with the Lavant here being joined by a contribution running down from the area of Cucumber Farm to the north. The 1962 guide to the parish churches of Singleton, West and East Dean refers to a spring of the Lavant in a marshy field just above the bridge, which in the 18th century was called The Fountain and was enclosed in some sort of stone basin, remains of which were visible in living memory. The line of this tributary is also marked by a low brick bridge in a field just north of the farm buildings.

In times past, the Lavant had an important role to play in this area. Again quoting Ian Serraillier, 'Before the sheep washing, the watergate half way to West Dean and the stoppers by the Post Office were closed to build up the water, and the road was fenced off with hurdles to hold back the sheep. Most shepherds used this sheep-wash in time to clean the wool before shearing. Up the lane past Ivy Cottage the sheep were penned in batches of twenty or so, then tossed into the river, scrubbed and ducked and released to swim downstream. Afterwards the farmers treated the shepherds at *The Horse and Groom.* There was no more sheep washing after World War I.'

A short distance further south from the cricket field are the remains of another of the Lavant's contributions to agriculture: two brick pillars, joined to the banks

3   The Lavant at Charlton.

4   Singleton Pond.

5   Sluice gate at Singleton.

6   The Lavant at West Dean Gardens.

on either side by low brick walls, leaving only a narrow passage for the water to run through. These are part of the sluice which was used in the past to divert the flow under the road, via a culvert which still exists, and on to the meadows on the east side of the road. The purpose was to flood the meadows in December for about three weeks, preventing frost damage; and again in spring for 24 hours at a time. The Rev. Arthur Young (1741-1820), who did so much to publicise good agricultural practice in this country, wrote: 'The river Lavant from the spring head at East Dean to Chichester irrigates between four and five hundred acres. In July from two to three tons of hay are mown per acre.' The ditches and sluices that formed part of this irrigation system can still be seen in the grounds of the Weald and Downland Museum at Singleton.

Soon after this point, the river crosses back under the A286, to the east side of the road, by a bridge which few people today probably notice. Mr. Fred Bennett has told me that at one time this was a hump-backed bridge, which he well remembers for the many tons of Tarmac it took to take out the dips on either side so that traffic could travel faster, instead of taking off over the humps. It now flows through the farmlands of the West Dean Estate—another area where the water was used to flood the meadows by means of sluice gates, passing West Dean House to enter the delightful ornamental gardens that are open to the public. The present house has been subjected to many changes over the years. It was designed by James Wyatt (as were Chichester's Assembly Rooms) but has been much altered and enlarged, so that it is now one of the largest flint structures in the country. While serving as a residential college for fostering and teaching a wide range of traditional arts and crafts, it still retains the character of a country house.

A full description of the gardens has been published by the Edward James Foundation, the trust which controls the whole estate of about 6,000 acres. Sufficient here to say that the Lavant forms an integral part of the design of those gardens, and that the noted garden designer, Gertrude Jekyll, was commissioned in 1895 to design the Water Garden section. One of its attractive features is the little spring which adds its contribution to the growing strength of the river.

The stream emerges from the Gardens under an opening in a flint wall, to run parallel with the village road of West Dean. Now almost devoid of traffic, this was once part of the highway from London to Chichester, before it was realigned during the period of the building of the present West Dean House in 1804. By now the Lavant is a few feet wide, and is spanned in this section by two bridges, the first a foot bridge of unusual construction. Tom Wright, in volume four of his book, *The Gardens of Britain* (1978), refers to pumice-lined bridges over the bed of the river. The lower bridge here is of brick, and is at the start of a walk leading to the Trundle. A rough pencilled notebook of 1857 among West Dean parish records in the County Record Office mentions an account for a new bridge over the Lavant. The matter was first referred to the appropriate landowners, but it was established that the road, from Broom Farm and East Lane, was a public highway. The account was for £36 5s., and was finally settled by a compromise, £13 being charged to the Highway Account and the rest coming from public subscription.

Chapter Four

On to East Lavant

THERE IS AN IDYLLIC DESCRIPTION of our little river's first few miles in an 18th-century anonymous poem. *The Historicall Account of the Rise and Progress of the Charlton Congress* describes the early history of the Charlton Hunt. As the Duke of Richmond noted on the flyleaf of the book, 'This was brought to me by a Porter in the beginning of February 1737'.

> Amidst the South Saxonian hills there runs
> A verdant fruitful vale in which, at once
> Four small and pretty villages are seen;
> Eastden, the one, does first supply the spring
> Whence silky Lavant takes his future course;
> Charlton next, the beauty of the four,
> From twenty chalky rills, fresh vigour adds;
> Then swiftly on, his force redoubled, he
> Through all the meadows, to Singleton does glide;
> More strength he there receives, then boldly runs,
> Till, less confin'd, he wider spreads his fame,
> And passing Lavant, there he takes his name.

As we have seen earlier, this last claim is not exactly true, since it is the river which gave its name to the village.

From here the Lavant runs quietly on through fields, including those of Preston Farm. The booklet on the Edward James Foundation (1981) tells us that this was famous in the 17th century for its water meadows, with traces of the original sluices and irrigation channels still remaining. At the point where the A286 and the B2141 Chilgrove roads meet is a small culvert, with a line of trees running eastward, marking a ditch that at times adds a modest contribution to the Lavant. Not that it is always so modest, as is shown by an essay in Lavant Village School's history of the village compiled in 1966. Trudy Tucker, one of the children, recorded that in 1937 occurred the worst flood for years. Nearly three miles of road between Chichester and Petersfield resembled a river. The stretch from Lavant to Chilgrove was a real handicap to motorists. She adds that the river had more recently been cleared of weeds and widened to prevent floods.

It has been observed that long after the Lavant has ceased its yearly course through Chichester, it can still be seen in this stretch from Singleton to Binderton. The reason for this was supplied to me by the Portsmouth Water Company, when I enquired as to that organisation's connection with the river. Just north of Mid Lavant there is a small pumping station from which it is licensed to extract 27

7   Sheepwash Lane at Lavant.

megalitres per day from three boreholes in the chalk. It will be seen that 27 million litres a day, that is 6,000,000 gallons, represents quite a loss in the amount of water on its way to the south.

During those periods when the operative area of the various authorities involved in the Lavant was much smaller than it is today, references to the river in their annual reports were more frequent and specific. For example, the report of the Sussex River Authority for the year ending March 1967 gives statistics for the amount of water licensed to be extracted for various purposes. 31,040 million gallons of surface water could be taken for spray irrigation. For underground sources the figures were as follows: Public supply— 3,678,000 gallons; Spray irrigation—12,511; Industry— 85,165; Agriculture other than spray irrigation— 29,472; Cooling—18,250; Other uses—182,766. I have been unable to obtain comparable figures for the present time.

In Mid Lavant will be found the site of one of those Domesday mills referred to earlier. Mill Lane (though not so signed) is the rough, chalky track on the east side of the A286 just south of the old Chichester-Midhurst railway bridge. At the bottom of the lane is a cottage which, on the side facing the stream, still retains features of a mill. The Goodwood Archives contain correspondence between the Rector of East Lavant, the Rev. Henry Legge, and the Duke of Richmond. He complained that, even when the mill was not working, the miller kept the water pent back, so that the marsh forming part of the glebe land was flooded, spoiling the grass. (Can he not have read Arthur Young?) The Duke asks his agent, 'My dear Valentine, do you know whether the miller has any right to do what he is doing?'; but, despite further exchanges, nothing conclusive seems to have been established. Whatever the cause of the glebe land being flooded, it is a fact that this area is marked by springs and marshes. Water oozes from the ground, and at any time of year anyone walking the public footpath from Binderton to Lavant is liable to get wet feet.

The name of the road which descends from Mid to East Lavant speaks for itself: Sheepwash Lane. Bernard Price's book *Changing Chichester* (1982) has a photograph of that operation, showing the wooden sluices in place across the river. This is another section where flooding often occurred in the past. To quote again from Trudy Tucker's school essay: 'At one time the rivulet used to flood regularly on to the Recreation Ground and most houses around that area most winters. In 1937 there was the worst flood for years. Cars had to be pulled out from the water by horses.'

She also recounts an amusing story of the village in the last century, which is best told in her own words. 'In the Lower Road is a flint bungalow that was once the school of a Dame. In 1870 she had twelve scholars, all boys. They were locked in the cellar for punishment. In this cellar home-made wine was kept in casks. As they were sent there often they decided to bring home-made straws in order to drink the wine. On one occasion several of them became drunk.'

I have been told that in 1911 the village school was closed for a whole year, partly due to flooding and partly due to a continuous epidemic of illness. I can find no documentary evidence for this, but the School Managers' Minute Book for February 1913 records that Mr. Young, the Headmaster, disinfected the school after the children's attack of sore throats, for which service he later received a gratuity of one and a half guineas. Local mothers believed that the prevalent diphtheria was caused when the bed of the Lavant dried up. As we shall see when we come to deal with the subject of public health in Chichester, there may well have been some truth in this belief.

Mrs. Daphne Horn, writing to me from Hunston, recalls the spring floods when the whole village green and both roads would be under water, with the water entering the Village Hall and several cottages. Even when the Lavant kept to its course, it could still be a source of danger. Her sister had a lucky escape during the last war, as she was cycling home in the dark from Summersdale. Coming to the bridge from the direction of Parkers Hill, she meant to turn left up Pook Lane (or Poke Lane, as it used to be called). Instead she went right and landed up in the former sheep wash, by a bridge leading to the old blacksmith's shop. Fortunately her cries were heard by a passing villager; her cycle was rescued later.

She was lucky to escape with a soaking. Others have been less fortunate. Mrs. Lambourne, whose father was herdsman at Church Farm, has told me that a little girl was drowned at Potmoor, up Marsh Lane, a fate which she and her sister risked as children when they would wade in the rushing stream, up to their necks, for a dare. It was a Sunday treat to get watercress there despite, as she says, the loads of frogs in the water.

Chapter Five

Fordwater and Graylingwell

A T EAST LAVANT a bridge carries the road over the river, on to Goodwood. When a new watermain was being laid in November 1939, just 2'6" below the floor of the river, it was found that over the years the Lavant bed had gradually risen, so that the invert level of the bridge was at least a foot below the adjacent river bed. This same bridge was the subject of correspondence between Lavant Parish Council and the County Surveyor in 1968, since local people considered that with no protection for pedestrians it was a potential danger. The County Surveyor felt he could not recommend any improvement to the bridge at the present time, but he proposed visiting the site to see whether it would be possible to provide additional signs and markings to draw attention to the difficulties. But the Parish Council persisted; they felt that at least a footbridge should be provided. After a further exchange of letters, the Surveyor finally agreed; a sum would be included in the estimates for the year 1969/70 for the provision of a footbridge, which now stands at the north side of the road, separate from traffic.

8 Below East Lavant road bridge.

9 The ford at Fordwater.

From this point, the Lavant wends its way roughly in a south-easterly direction, skirting Church Farm, past the sewage works, to Fordwater. Again on this stretch there were sluices to divert the stream on to water meadows; here too was the 'Six Foot' pool, a popular spot for swimming. For many years Fordwater was on the coach road from Chichester to London. The ford was not a simple crossing from bank to bank; the road ran for quite a considerable distance along the bed of the river itself, as can still be seen from the adjoining footpath. Having survived this experience, passengers would soon be driven through East Lavant for the hazardous, bumpy ride up Chalkpit Lane before the descent, via Town Lane, to Singleton. There is no longer a through road here, but a pleasant footpath from the Lavant-Strettington road, and the river is now crossed by a footbridge. Formerly this was a simple wooden footbridge, but this has been replaced by a substantial structure capable of carrying traffic to the nearby farm.

With the appropriately named Winterbourne Road above its right bank, the Lavant continues its way east of Graylingwell Hospital, to Westhampnett. This is a convenient point to consider some wider aspects of water supply as it affected Chichester, since the Lavant is just one of many sources in this area, either surface or underground. In the grounds of Bishop Otter College, at the side of the playing field close to the footpath on the east side of College Lane, is an arched brickwork cover to an old well, one of the sources of water for the city of Chichester in earlier times. In the City Museum in Little London is the lead filter of Roman origin found at the bottom of this well, which was attached to a lead pipe. The line of this pipe was down the side of College Lane, across what is now Oaklands Park finally

10   The Grayling Well.

to St Martin's Square, to feed a stand pipe there. Dr. Elizabeth Murray, formerly the Principal of the College, has recalled the time in the 1950s when there used to be an open stream down the west side of College Lane, known locally as the River Otter. Water used to collect in a pond or pit known as Dell Hole, now the car park opposite *The Hope* public house.

In 1864 a well, fifty feet deep, was dug at Graylingwell Farm, to serve the new hospital; two wells were recorded in 1928. The original structure can still be seen in the grounds. A few years ago, it was an attractive rustic building of flint with a tiled roof, its wrought iron gate bearing the name GRAYLING WELL. It is now a sad sight, a victim of time and neglect; overgrown with bushes, the roof tumbling in, and an ominous warning that it is now in a dangerous condition.

Chapter Six

Westhampnett

O N 21 JULY 1941, the South West River Catchment Board began to carry out work to deepen the channel of the Lavant, from a point west of Fordwater Copse, as far as Old Place Farm, Westhampnett. The object was to construct a tank trap, which was undertaken by order of the War Department under Defence Regulation no. 50. Fortunately for Chichester, its efficiency was never called into question. It was not long, however, before questions *were* being asked. The Land Drainage Records for that period include a considerable correspondence extending from February 1943 to December 1944, on the question of ultimate compensation which might be due to the various bodies affected. These included the Catchment Board itself, the owners of farms adjoining the river, the Graylingwell Hospital authorities, and Sadler and Company as freeholders of the river bed itself. The extent of the works was quite considerable. A photograph taken in February 1944 shows Mr. E.V. Dawe, the manager of Sadler's mill, standing in the dry bed of the Lavant, with the sides of the banks way above his head; the water had drained through the gravel bottom. In the end, it was decided that reinstatement should be restricted to some minor bulldozing of the banks, and, possibly under some pressure, everyone involved finally agreed to waive any claim for financial compensation.

This mill at Westhampnett is a successor to the one recorded in the Domesday survey. For many years it was known as Burnt Mill, presumably a reference to an earlier fire. In the deed of 1659, the name is applied both to the water mill and to a windmill close by. Much more recently—in 1906—the mill was again severely damaged by fire. The cost of replacing the machinery amounted to more than £2,250. The work of repairing the building itself ran from June to November of that year, and the Building Account Wages Book shows that the total bill for scaffolders, carpenters, bricklayers, labourers and the foreman totalled £620 14s. 3d. The miller at that time was another member of the Sadler family, Henry.

Like many other properties in and around Chichester, the mill was owned by the Duke of Richmond, being rented to successive members of the same family. In 1856 Robert Sadler was having difficulties, owing to lack of water coming from the Lavant, even though five years earlier a steam engine had been installed to work the mill. It needed about 1,200 gallons of water for a full day's operation, and during the previous five months he had only been able to run the engine on 21 days. So he asked the Duke to make a reduction in his rent. During that time water for malting had to be obtained from nearby brick kilns. In the 1930s, power was supplied by a turbine engine, which also provided power for some limited electric lighting. At weekends, and other times when the mill was not in operation, a small Petter engine was used.

11   Westhampnett Mill.

12   Sluice for Westhampnett Mill.

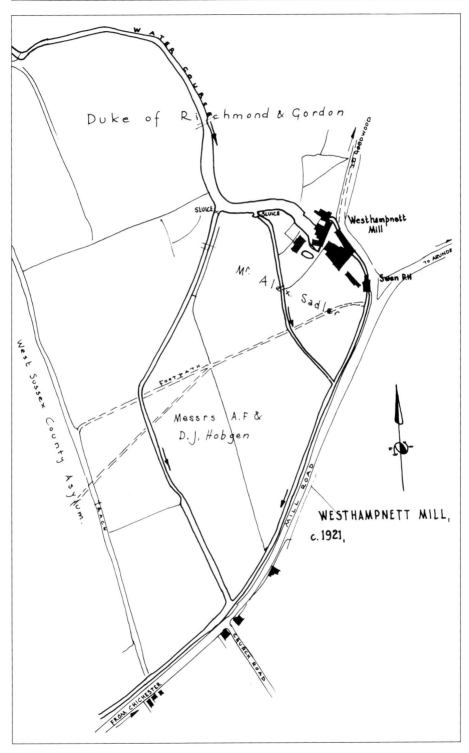

13 Plan: Westhampnett Mill, *c*.1921.

In 1918 the Duke decided to sell the property. His tenant at that time was Alexander Sadler, and he would have much preferred to remain as a tenant, but he had no choice in the matter. Negotiations went ahead surprisingly quickly. Sadler asked that a small cottage on the Chichester Road, sublet to George Privett, should be included in the deal, and that he should have access to the sluices to the north of the property, since they were essential to his business. Finally these, and the field which they bounded, were included in the transaction, the purchase price being £5,000.

It will be seen from a plan of the area that at this stage the Lavant has been divided into three streams, controlled by sluices. We shall meet the main stream again shortly as it joins the Westhampnett Road, but the water feeding the mill pond was subjected to yet another of the many diversions suffered by our little river. The easterly stream flowed into the pond and worked the mill, later running under the old *Swan* public house, before that was resited as part of the present motel complex. When there was a surplus of water, the excess was diverted into the middle of the three streams by a second sluice. A system of water gates also allowed the river to be used to flood the water meadows nearby, a process which we noted earlier in its course. These fields, lying roughly between the mill and the crematorium grounds, are still often waterlogged in places. Roads adjacent to these fields bear appropriate names: Conduit Mead, Millfield Close, The Water Plat.

To conclude the story of Westhampnett Mill: Sadler and Company continued the business as millers, corn merchants and maltsters into the 1930s. From 1938 to 1954 local directories describe the business as dog cake and poultry food manufacturers, until the firm moved to the industrial estate on Terminus Road. In 1968, the mill is shown as occupied by Weston Foods, who were followed by Charta Furniture Limited. The site is now (2000) residential housing.

Chapter Seven

Nearing Chichester

WHAT REMAINS OF THE LAVANT PROPER, as it were, emerges from hedges on the Westhampnett Road opposite the end of Church Road, to run alongside the road in a south-westerly direction. But it has not always done so. For it was roughly in this area (it is difficult to be specific with such a wayward river) that the Lavant suffered its most dramatic change of direction. Historians are themselves divided as to the period, or even the cause; one theory suggests that it took place in medieval times, the other favours the Roman period. What is agreed is that at some early time in history the Lavant continued roughly in the line which we have followed so far and made its way to the sea via Pagham Rife and Pagham Harbour. As for the reason for the man-made change, one suggestion is that it was to drain the marshy area to the south of Chichester; but Barry Cunliffe and others consider that it was part of the Roman plan to protect the city, in association with their construction of the walls.

Back to modern times: in 1939 the West Sussex River Catchment Board was in dispute with the West Sussex County Council. On 22 August the Board wrote: 'It appears that the weight of traffic on the County road is causing the bank of the main river to collapse, and the County Council from time to time in repairing the bank has encroached upon the course of the river, as much as four feet in the last ten years. The whole of the bank immediately adjacent to the A27 along the front of Pound Farm Gravel Pit requires to be reconstructed, by means of a concrete retaining wall.'

But the Board did not get much satisfaction in the matter. There was no reply till 18 January in the following year, when the County Surveyor explained that the delay was due to 'dealing with more urgent, war matters'. He considered the Board's case unproved. He did not see the slightest need for a concrete wall; any changes were due to scouring by the river itself. Hall and Company's gravel pit was on the site of the present crematorium. In the 1950s, the firm diverted and sandbagged the stream in order to prevent flooding of the pit.

Despite its normal placid behaviour, the Lavant has in its time been responsible for several deaths by drowning. The 'wild impetuous course' of Crocker's poem has sometimes taken on a deadly significance. I have been told of a girl being drowned at Potmoor, at Lavant; of two girls losing their lives near Mount Lane, Chichester, in the 1920s; of a death by drowning in a garden along Market Avenue; but details are often lacking. One particular case, however, is well documented. This quotation (in near breathless prose) comes from *The Brighton Herald* for 24 May 1828. 'On the afternoon of Thursday se'night, as a poor old man seventy years of age, an inhabitant of Boxgrove, between which village and Chichester he had acted as common carrier for some years, was leaving the latter place on his return home, with a little cart and pony, and being, as it stated, in a state of intoxication on his arrival at the bridge leading to Graylingwell, the animal, being blind, went into the Lavant course, so it is supposed, wanting to drink, dragging the cart and owner after it. The water being very deep at this spot the pony was drowned from the weight of the cart pressing on it. But assistance arriving, the driver was rescued. He was found to have received such considerable injuries that he was carried to the Hospital where he died on Monday evening.'

There are several footbridges across the river on the north side of Westhampnett Road; one of them, of brick construction, leads north in the direction of Graylingwell, by a footpath now littered with household debris. The stream now runs between the main road and Story Road on the housing estate with wide rushy margins on either side. It was here, a few years ago, that the District Council proposed to culvert the Lavant in order to take in further land for housing. Fortunately, as many people will consider, the scheme was not carried out. So much of the Lavant has already been covered over in its passage through Chichester that any potential threat is strongly resisted by local amenity organisations.

In 1960/1, as a measure to prevent flooding in St Pancras, the West Sussex River Board constructed a wall, 500 feet long, at a cost of £545.

Chapter Eight

St Pancras: Flooding

S TANDING BACK FROM THE MAIN ROAD a few yards further along is a small thatched cottage, built of an attractive mixture of brick, stone and rubble. An inscribed stone on the facade records that 'Here are the sacred remains of St James's Hospital which was founded in the reign of Henry the First for the reception of persons afflicted with leprosy.' This was the ancient Hospital of St Mary Magdalen and St James. Chichester's Bishop Story, who built the Market Cross, left 3s. 4d. to the hospital in his will. A later bishop, Seffrid, gave 80 acres of land at Colworth for the same cause, and the hospital also owned land at Portfield. Leprosy disappeared from this country by the beginning of the 16th century, and by 1690 there was little income for the hospital in its new role of almshouse. In that year the Master, Mr. Peter Edge, Rector of St Pancras, noted that there was only one inmate, 'and she is a miserable idiot'. Later occupants were more fortunate, and actually *asked* to stay there. A curious entry in the records of the Board of Guardians says that Mr. Nowland had requested that St James's house might be granted to him 'to air his relations'; similarly that Mr. Halsted should have the use of the house 'to air himself in'.

14   St James's Hospital.

The original building was burned down in 1781, and the commemorative plaque was placed on the present cottage a few years later by the Rev. William Walker, at one time Master of the Hospital.

When Swanfield Drive was under construction, this involved the disturbance of the former burial ground of the hospital. The bones so disturbed were reinterred in the Litten ground off New Park Road in October 1947; a stone commemorates the fact. More skeletons were unearthed in 1986 prior to housing development off Story Road; these remains of the victims of leprosy are being studied by specialists at Bradford University who are researching this disease.

The drawing of St James's Hospital was published in *The Gentleman's Magazine* for July 1792, only a few years after the disastrous fire. The accompanying letter, from 'S' of Whyke, claims that it is an exact representation, 'done by one who was never instructed in the first principles of that beautiful art'. He goes on to say, 'If we may judge from the ruins, it was a very plain building. It now serves as a cottage for a poor family. In the background is seen Bow, or Four Barrows, Hill, so called from the four large barrows on the ridge of a high hill.'

At one time there was a deep depression on the west side of the building, into which the Lavant flowed to form a leper's pool in which the inmates could bathe. In 1888 the Medical Officer of Health reported that the Scavengers Field at St James and the old hole close to it, both washed by the Lavant as it enters the city, were in a most objectionable state calculated to greatly discredit the place in the eyes of visitors and others. The gardens of the cottages at the corner of Spitalfields Lane and Westhampnett Road form quite a depression today, and I believe this marks the site of the former leper pool.

At this point, the river crosses under the Westhampnett Road to the south side where, a few years ago, a small child was rescued from drowning after falling into the river and being swept under the bridge. Here, opposite Spitalfields Lane (the name commemorates the ancient hospital) stands St James's Post, an obelisk which once marked the eastern boundary of the city of Chichester. It bears the inscription 'Erected in the Mayoralty of Charles Duke of Richmond Lennox Aubigny 1745'. The city boundaries were extended in 1891 and again in 1893. There had been an earlier monument at this spot 'to the honour of Our Lord Jesus Christ and in the likeness of the Holy Cross, called St Jamys Cross'. On 3 March 1547, at about eleven o'clock at night, it was dug up and overthrown by two men hoping to find treasure there. In view of the gravity of their offence it is surprising to read that the men, Andrew Drewett, a weaver from Petworth, and John Lane, a Fishbourne miller, were pardoned 'for the said felony without fee or fine'.

A minute of the City Council meeting held on 11 March 1740 ordered that six or more of the Common Council were to view the repair of St James's Bridge, and later entries show more repairs being necessary. As mentioned earlier, the Domesday record includes a mill at Chichester, and it seems clear that it was located along this next stretch of the river. James Spershott (1710-89), whose invaluable Memoirs were published as No. 30 of the *Chichester Papers* (now out of print), says that '1763 ... The watermill at the cast end of St Pancras taken down'. The Council minutes of 18 April 1803 record that the proprietor of the site of the watermill called King's Mill otherwise Lavant Mill and the cottages and buildings erected thereon has applied to renew the lease of the same. In October of the same year,

15   The Lavant at Riverside, St Pancras.

Dr. Thomas Sanden's lease was sealed as mortgagee of the properties for forty years on payment of £11 13s. 0d.

In August 1849, there was a serious fire at the nearby Florance (*sic*) Brewery in St Pancras. This may have been the present Lion House on the north side of the road, bearing the date 1783. The bridge over the Lavant was known in the past as Florance's Bridge. Charles Jacques, who lived in the Hornet, wrote in his scrap book: 'The salvation of the dwelling house is mainly attributed to the bountiful supply of water from Mr. Knott's mill pond, the watercourse running in front of the property in question.' Nowadays, there would be little hope of the river being used for such a purpose in the month of August.

The City Council minutes of 10 November 1879 record the enfranchisement to Edward Habin of the scite (*sic*) only of the Water Mill called the King's Mill otherwise Lavant Mill, and also the Mill Pond and dashing pool: 'the said Water Mill having for many years been fallen into great decay and taken down'. Together with three tenements or cottages occupied by various tenants, the properties were conveyed to Habin for £73, with the rights being reserved to the Mayor, Aldermen and Citizens to the bed of the stream itself, together with access, and the right to cleanse, dig, etc. (being the normal formula).

Spershott records that in 1768 'The River Lavant, where it used to run across the main road to the edge of Portfield, was turned to the north side of the road to St James's, and there a new bridge built'. In 1832, following one of the many surveys of the river, the City Council ordered the repairing of the Bridge over the Lavant Course in St Pancras; in 1854 more work was needed—the carpenter's account was for five shillings, with a further 10s. 6d. the following year. In September

1879, the Council's sights were set much higher. The Highways and Paving Committee, having considered the desirability of making a road from this bridge in St Pancras to the Oving Road and Portfield, recommended that a new bridge be built to replace the existing wooden structure, of sufficient strength for carriages to pass over. The Committee added the proviso: that the owners of the land on the Oving side should make and dedicate to the public a proper and sufficient carriage road through their land from the bridge to the Oving Road. Faced with such a suggestion, it is not surprising that the landowners took no such action. As a result what would today be a most useful addition to the local road pattern is still a vehicular cul-de-sac formed by Green Lane and Bridge Road, while the bridge itself is still restricted to pedestrian use.

At this point, the river turns left to run between houses, including the former *Star and Garter* public house in St Pancras, and the Riverside bungalows on its left bank, to form one of the most picturesque stretches in its passage through Chichester, and continuing south of the Newell Centre and under the road bridge of Tozer Way. However, at one time the line of the river was much closer to the main road. In 1985, when Southern Gas workmen were digging a hole a few yards from the St Pancras footpath, they discovered a much deeper hole, and were told by a local resident who had known the Lavant all her life that this marked the former line of the river. In earlier times, it just skirted the corner of the former St Pancras School before making a sharp left and a right to continue behind the former malthouse of Lambert and Norris and along the bottom of the gardens of houses on the south side of St Pancras. The stream is visible again from the bridge on the private road which passes through Rowe's premises between St Pancras and the Hornet, and again on the east side of the Needlemakers stretch of the Ring Road. From then on, its passage becomes increasingly unattractive, until it disappears just east of the Unicorn building (now Minerva Court) in Eastgate Square.

This section of the Lavant was in times past one of the worst areas affected by flooding, and this is often mentioned in contemporary records. Spershott's entry for 1771 is as follows: 'The new bridge built over the Lavant without the East Gate before which the water lies open, spread wide and, when the springs were high, flow'd [i.e. flooded] from within a few yards of East Gate into the Hornet as far as the Poor House, and was so deep in the current that I have seen it above the beds of the waggons. There was then only a narrow bridge of two stone arches from the Hornet to the Pancras for horse and foot people.' Perhaps it was this same set of arches that was the subject of complaint in April 1627 when, at the City Court Leet and View of Frankpledge, the Grand Jury presented that the Steward 'suffereth the Stonen Brigg without the East Gate is verie much decayed', also that 'the Grate of the South Walls is verie much at faulte and stoppeth the water, that passengers cannot passe by that way'.

James Spershott died in 1789, but in the notebook containing his memoirs there are entries in a different hand for the years 1797 to 1809. This last year includes the following note: 'February. The water of the Lavant run all round the city occasioned by its overflowing its banks which flowed the lower rooms in St Pancras and the Hurnet. Run rapidly into the lane to St Michael's Fair Field [i.e. New Park Road], so into the Lighten [The Litten] and flowed the Bishop's Garden Field [the present Jubilee Gardens] and found its way round to the North

16   Floods at New Park Road, pre-1887.

Gate as in the year 1763, which may be expected once in 50 years.' This is in fact word for word the same as Spershott himself recorded in 1763, save for his comment, 'as in 1713, just 50 years before, and if periodical may again be expected in 1813'.

The *Brighton Herald* for 19 January 1826 reported that the continuance of wet weather caused the Lavant at Chichester to overflow its banks, but providentially no injury or inconvenience was sustained 'except that of filling the cellars of more than half the houses in the city'. No doubt their inhabitants considered that this was inconvenience enough. There was more serious trouble a week later. 'The inundations in the neighbourhood of Chichester from the overflowing of the Lavant have considerably subsided ... During the past week, and on Monday night, some persons cut a channel from the Lavant watercourse across Snag Lane [roughly on the line of the present Stirling Road—see chapter IX] at the entrance to Fletcher's Field in the parish of St Pancras, whereby the water was diverted from its regular course and flowed into parts of Kingsham Farm in the occupation of Messrs. J. and T. Hayllar, which in a few hours carried off an immense body of water. A reward of ten pounds has been offered for the discovery of the offenders. It has been generally thought that this was part of the original course and, but a few years since, passengers had to cross a wooden bridge on this very spot to get to the fields.' As we shall see when we look at Kingsham, there was some truth in this belief.

Continuing the saga of Lavant floods in this area, Charles Austen Jacques (1792-1872) of Hornet House, Chichester, noted in his Chronicles of Chichester 1066-1872 (*sic*) that 'in the last week of December 1839 the Hornet and the road without West Gate were inundated by the Lavant overflowing, occasioned by the almost continuous rains of the preceding year. Again in December 1852, the Lavant overflowed its banks and inundated the Pancras and the Hornett. The road by Dell

Hole and Franklin Place was also flooded. There had been almost incessant rain for almost six weeks.'

On 11 November 1894, when a hundred yards of the Hornet were flooded, local landowner, Mr. E.T. Habin, made several vehicles available for public use so that local inhabitants, particularly the schoolchildren from Portfield and Whyke, could get into the city. For this service, he was thanked by the Council at its December meeting. But none of this softened his reaction to their request that workmen should enter his field to arch over the Lavant at the back of his premises. It was recorded that 'Mr. Habin declines to allow persons across the field, and protests against covering the Lavant Course', half of which belonged to him. The actual location of this property is not clear, but it is surprising if in fact the Corporation had not retained the rights of access to, and work on, the river. (See page 23 for Habin's acquisition of the site of the Town Mill.)

The problem has continued into our own times. When repairs were being carried out to the road bridge at East Lavant in 1939, the South West Sussex River Catchment Board noted 'the need to deal with flooding at St Pancras before any floodwater is released at Lavant'. Again, in December 1960, the *Chichester Observer* reported as follows: 'Wearing rubber boots and armed with buckets and mops, shopkeepers and householders in St Pancras have been anxiously watching the water level in the River Lavant. Many have been hard hit by the flow which burst from the Lavant after the gale, rising above sandbagging and pouring into the cellars, kitchens, shops and showrooms. Between 25 and 30 workmen from the West Sussex River Board and the City Council piled sandbags in a wall beside the Lavant and against doors, front gates and cellar grids in an attempt to keep houses dry. For the first time in memory, it poured over the footbridge from St Pancras to Green Lane, and workmen had to build a wooden plank bridge across it on sandbags.'

James Spershott's associations with the Lavant continue. As he says in his introduction to the Memoirs, he lived in the Manor House of Rumbolds Whyke, close adjoining the Lavant near the East Gate of the city of Chichester. A joiner by trade, he was ordained joint pastor of the Baptist Chapel, built in 1728. This is the present-day Eastgate Hall in Market Road, in a corner of the Cattle Market area. Close by was a pool, fed by the Lavant, which was used for open-air baptisms. In Eastgate Square itself for many centuries the Lavant formed a large pond, the receptacle for rubbish from houses in and around the Square—a fate which the river was to suffer increasingly as time went on, as described in a later chapter.

From this point on, until it re-emerges beyond the city walls, much of the Lavant runs below ground in brick culverts. To earlier generations of Cicestrians, these formed a tempting challenge, and many tales are told of exploration and escapades along the river bed. One of the most hazardous must have been the trip downstream by way of a polystyrene raft, which nearly ended in disaster. The youthful crew had to be rescued when their voyage ended abruptly at an unsuspected grille below the surface.

Chapter Nine

To Kingsham and Round the Walls

THOUGH THE NAME SNAG LANE has long since disappeared from the Chichester street scene, it was of some importance in the documentation of the Lavant. It was on a line outside the city wall, roughly from Eastgate Square to the present Caledonian Road/Stirling Road corner, then southwards to lead to Kingsham Farm, a line followed by one of the many branches of the river. Little remains of the buildings there—a few brick walls and an ornamental stone arch in the grounds of the Boys' High School, now overshadowed by the Texaco Garage. This is all that is left of the former Manor House and even earlier, the King's Hame, allegedly a Saxon royal palace. *Kelly's Directory* for Sussex (1890) says that in earlier times when the king paid a visit to Kingsham he was presented, under the custom of petty serjeanty, with a skein of thread for his crossbow, but it should perhaps be added that the *Victoria County History of Sussex* casts some doubt on this suggestion of Kingsham as a royal manor. The same authority, in 1973, expressed the vain hope that 'such remains of the old building as have been preserved will still probably be kept free from modern development ...'

Dallaway's *History of the Western Division of the County of Sussex* (1815) states that the manor was originally surrounded by a moat connected with the nearby Lavant, which by his time had been filled in and enclosed by a quadrangular wall. As one explores this area today, it is possible to imagine that some of the arches under those walls may mark the line of that moat.

The prevalence of water in this area is reflected in the name Watery Lane almost opposite the Kingsham Farm site, and the continuous flow of water into the east side of the canal from under the High School playing field.

The course of the Lavant through, or rather round, the city is shown in several of the early maps of Chichester. John Norden's map of 1595 not only depicts its meandering path from the East Gate area, around the walls to the south and west, but adds the comment that the city 'is washed on every side except the north by the little river Lavant, the course of which stream is very unaccountable, being sometimes quite dry but at other times, and that very often in the midst of Summer, so full as to run with some violence'. John Speed in 1610 (based on Norden) and William Gardner's *Accurate Plan of the City of Chichester* 1769 show much the same line of the Lavant. They all show the bridge known as Squitry Bridge where it passed under the lane which later became our present Orchard Street. In addition, Gardner's map clearly shows its passage under buildings at the junction of St Pancras and The Hornet, together with the open pond in Eastgate Square referred to above. What is perhaps surprising is that three other early maps—that of 1723 by William Stukeley, Emanuel Bowen's (again 'accurate') map of 1749 and John Rocque in

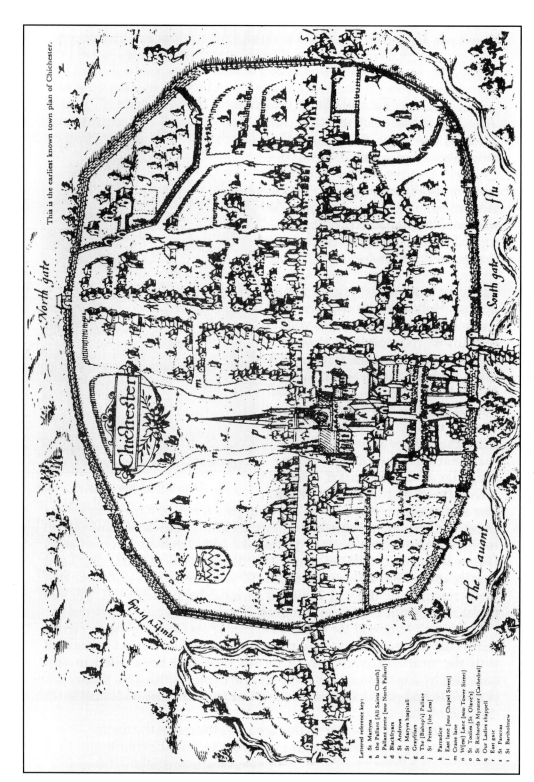

This is the earliest known town plan of Chichester.

North gate

South gate

The Lauant

Flu.

Spitle Feild

Chichester

17   John Norden's map of Chichester, 1595.

18 Section of culvert under Eastgate Square.

19 The garden of 'Market Walls', in Market Avenue.

20   Culverting under Market Road.

1764—have the river turning sharply south as soon as it runs under the South Gate, with no indication of its further passage around the south-west walls. But wherever the Lavant is shown, it must have been clearly visible at the time.

Snag Lane, referred to earlier, is frequently mentioned in the Council minutes of the last century. There were a few cottages adjoining the Lavant, and one section of the bank was leased to the Duke of Richmond. In September 1842, the Town Clerk wrote to the Duke's Steward complaining of the state of the fences there. The Duke's solicitors countered that in their opinion His Grace was not liable for their repair. In fact the dispute ended in a compromise over the cost of the work. Before the opening of the Cattle Market in 1872 and the creation of Market Avenue, only a footpath existed.

1887 was the year of Queen Victoria's Golden Jubilee. One old Cicestrian, William Hoare by name, marked the occasion by compiling his reminiscences of the city over the previous 70 years. They are written in the form of an imaginary conversation between 'William Young' and 'Old Age'. The writing is naive, often illiterate as he had little education, but the work makes fascinating reading. The original is in the County Record Office. There are several references to the Lavant. For instance: 'Where the new Market Road is now, used to be a field. On the left side of that road was a path that led from the Basin Road to Eastgate Square. Beyond the path and the old city wall, there was what is called the Lavant course. A part of that was exposed to the view of passers-by, which was not very pleasant at times; but when the New Market Road was made it was closed in and a wall built round as you see it now.'

This is by no means the last we shall hear of the unpleasant side of the Lavant in the 19th century.

Chapter Ten

Under the City

TODAY MUCH OF ITS JOURNEY THROUGH CHICHESTER is hidden from view and many people seem to be unaware that the odd stretches of open water that seasonally make a brief appearance are in fact manifestations of our river. Having passed under Eastgate Square, it now follows a curving line under Market Road and the garden of Friary Close at the end of Friary Lane, to emerge in the beautiful garden of the house known as Market Walls, in Market Avenue. It continues through the adjoining garden of Riverside Lodge and through a small open space owned by the District Council—a tangle of Japanese knotweed and small trees, an oasis of green behind its railings, in which the purling stream can just be glimpsed.

At one time a flood relief pipe ran along the line of Basin Road, to carry surplus water into the Canal Basin while the river itself was visible again for a short spell as it ran through a small pond to the south of the present Old Market Avenue, a spot now covered over in the area surrounding Christ Church. The Lavant now continues, as it did then, under Southgate, south of the *Fountain Inn,* to emerge beyond what is now part of a car park. Of the South Gate itself, nothing can now be seen. The city gates were taken down between 1772 and 1783, but one of the bastions on the south side remained until 1803, when George Gatehouse applied to build a wall on the Lavant bank opposite his tenement and garden outside the South Gate, having secured a 40 year lease on the property. The City Council gave him permission to take down and use the materials of the bastion which stood in part of the garden, 'on condition that the wall be four feet above the footpath, fourteen inches thick above the path, and eighteen inches beneath it, and that it shall be built with sufficient quoins, not less than ten, to support it.' So much for planning regulations being a modern invention!

A few years later, disaster struck William Kenwood's grocery shop in Southgate, as the *Brighton Herald* reported on 20 March 1823: 'On Saturday night the floor of the shop fell into the river Lavant, the arch over which, suddenly giving way, precipitated flour, sugar, lard, plums, bacon and most of the moveables of the shop into the stream beneath. Fortunately no one was in the shop at the time to share the same fate.' In the following December, Mr. Kenwood submitted a claim to the Council for his loss sustained in cleaning the watercourse under his house, and it was resolved that the Mayor with two others should investigate and report on the matter. He eventually received £15 compensation.

To return to the course of the Lavant: just outside the above-mentioned car park, the stream makes a sharp bend from west to south, and a few yards further on it has been divided. While the main stream runs westerly below the city wall with a meadow to the right and the Prebendal School playing field to the left,

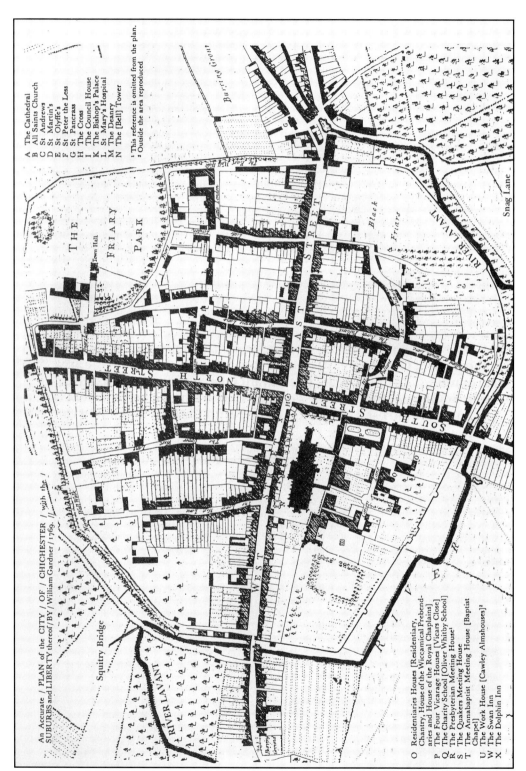

A The Cathedral
B All Saints Church
C St Andrews
D St Martin's
E St Olyffe's
F St Peter the Less
G St Pancrass
H The Cross
I The Council House
K The Bishop's Palace
L St Mary's Hospital
M The Deanry
N The [Bell] Tower

[1] This reference is omitted from the plan.
[2] Ouside the area reproduced

An Accurate / PLAN of the CITY / OF / CHICHESTER / with the / SUBURBS and LIBERTY thereof / BY / William Gardner 1769. //

O Residentiaries Houses [Residentiary
  Chantry, House of the Wiccamical Prebend-
  aries and House of the Royal Chaplains]
P The Four Vicarage Houses [Vicars Close]
Q The Charity School [Oliver Whitby School]
R The Presbyterian Meeting House[1]
S The Quakers Meeting House
T The Annabaptist Meeting House [Baptist
  Chapel]
U The Work House [Cawley Almshouses][2]
W The Swan Inn
X The Dolphin Inn

21   William Gardner's map of Chichester, 1769.

another overflow, controlled by a sluice gate, carries southward almost to the railway station before another right turn, to continue beside the Avenue de Chartres car park and the Westgate Leisure Centre. In the spring of 1986, our patient Lavant suffered yet another diversion, to avoid the Leisure Centre complex. The water was shut off at the Southgate sluice gate while this work was carried out. The possibility of shutting off this section permanently was considered, but the Southern Water Authority decided to keep the channel in existence as a precaution against future flooding. In view of the amount of rubbish with which this stretch is often de-spoiled, this might not have been too serious a loss. One day in July 1985, a party of volunteers removed 27 sacks of litter from one small section here, a worthwhile achievement, but nothing to the 30 tons of debris cleared from the culverted section in the city in 1957.

Back to the main stream—a very pleasant walk when the water is running. I have seen a water vole swimming here, and early in 1985 surprised a heron as it stood on the bank. More noteworthy, however, must be the presence of fish here, as recorded by the *Brighton Gazette* for 24 February 1825. 'On Saturday last a fine trout was caught in that part of the river Lavant which runs through the garden of Colonel Brereton under the walls of the south part of the city. The fish was taken by the gardeners. It weighed upwards of 4lbs and was 22 inches in length; three others were observed in company but they decamped.' As the paper rightly comments, 'when we consider that this river is dry for four or five months of the year, the circumstances are worthy of notice'.

The *Victoria County History of Sussex,* volume 3, records that the Dean of Chichester once owned lands and orchards between the city walls and the Lavant. At some date between 1178 and 1180, he obtained a licence from Henry II to make a postern gate through the wall. This gate, says *V.C.H.*, is clearly recognisable in the Dean's garden. It is surprising to see that, on the 1890 Ordnance Survey map of the city, reproduced in David Butler's *The Town Plans of Chichester, 1595-1898*—a most interesting and informative collection—the flow of the river is arrowed towards the south-east, which is entirely the wrong direction.

One old Cicestrian has told me that the Westgate Fields had their own flood gates, and were regularly flooded in winter and spring. Cattle were unloaded at the railway sidings, to be fattened for the market on the lush herbage. Three graziers are recorded in the Chichester section of Bailey's *British Directory* for the year 1784.

Chapter Eleven

Beating the Bounds

A S THE EARLY MAPS SHOW, for centuries the Lavant continued its protective circuit of the city walls to a point roughly half way along their western section before making a sharp bend to the south-west, on its way to the sea. The point at which it was crossed by a track outside the walls is marked as Squitry Bridge, a significant sounding name which, however, does not appear in any of my dictionaries. The track, subsequently road, was known as Squitry Lane, later refined to Scuttery Lane, and was on the line of the present Orchard Street. The name is perpetuated in the house Little Scuttery at No.9 Orchard Street. The old line of the stream skirted the Pentecostal Chapel, along the south-east boundary of the new car park and the site of the new County Record Office (until recently part of the school playing fields), alongside Henty's Brewery, under Westgate, to the former tannery on the south of that road. During this short stretch the Lavant was joined by other waters coming down from the north, including a drainage ditch from a meadow at the North Gate, the Campus—though 'Campis' is often the form found in the City records. Although the river itself no longer takes this circuitous course, fresh water is still to be found; in fact the owner of No.5 Orchard Street demonstrated this by drawing a bucketful for me from the well at the bottom of his garden, which he said he had never known to run dry.

Old William Hoare, in his 1887 Jubilee reminiscences, has quite a bit to say about this field. 'Many years ago, where the allotments are now at West Orchard Street, there was a cottage adjoining and belonging to that meadow. An old man lived in this cottage by the name of Potter. He had a small dairy of three or four cows which he used to keep in the meadow. That is why it went by the name of Potters Field. The cottage has long since been pulled down and a substantial house built on the spot where the cowshed stood. And I daresay you have noticed that it is called Potter Villa.' Passers-by today will see that the house, with its inscribed stone 'Potters Villa / T L P / 1883' stands there still, at the entrance to the twitten leading to Parchment Street.

Hoare continues: 'There were no circuses as there are in these days. There were what was called Montebacks [*sic*]. When they came to Chichester they used to stay for a week or ten days; they always went to the Potters Field. They used to make a ring with posts and ropes. When the performances were over they took the horses away and brought into the ring lots of common things, such as tea trays, clocks, crockery ware, knives and forks, calico prints, as prizes for raffles for which they sold tickets. That was the way they were paid for their performances.'

The Lavant had its part to play in the operations both of the brewery and the tanyard, and the acquisition of adjoining land could be an advantage. Alderman

George Henty was one of the many councillors to whom land in the ownership of the City Council was enfranchised. He was Mayor in 1858, though he was not present at the meeting that year which granted him the two acres of land 'without the West Gate, near Scuttery Bridge, called Scuttery—the Lavant Course or Stream running on the east side, and lands belonging to the Lord Bishop of Chichester on the west side; save and except a small piece of land whereon a Chapel and other buildings have been erected.' Subject to certain conditions as to access by the Corporation, the conveyance was agreed and sealed and the sum of £78 paid for the transaction.

One of the river Lavant's functions in earlier days was to define the boundaries of the ancient city for a considerable part of their length. These boundaries are set out in great detail at the beginning of one of the City Council minute books covering the 18th century. The record is dated 26 May 1769, and shows how limited were the confines of Chichester at that time. The line proceeded from 'Bound Stone' No.1 at the South Gate, by a pollard elm on the Lavant bank, along the bank on the south side of the stream to a close called Scotch Croft (No.2) and across the Lavant. It then went through the back window of the *White Horse* ale house, through the building and out of a window at the front (No.3) thence (No.4) along the west side of the Lavant Course to Scuttery Bridge (No.5)—in other words, between the south-western walls and the present Orchard Street. The boundary then extended northward across the 'Broil' and round to stone No.23 at St James's Hospital and straight on to the Obelisk in the Highway from Chichester to Hampnett, to cross the stream once more and continue along the bank to the Guilden Field (No.24), east along the Lavant bank for about forty yards to stone No.25 on the corner of a house 'heretofore Farrendens now Cobdens' and eastwards to No.26 at the corner of a tenement of Mr. William Knott 'heretofore known by the Name of Town Mill'. The boundary then continued along the north bank back to the Obelisk at St James's. After a further section we pick up the river again at No.37, where we are told to 'keep the Lavant Course close on the right till you come to No.38 upon the bank of the Water Course and near the gate and stile leading to the Pond Field into the same Field along the path called Jack a Lanthorns Path and thence to the Bound Stone first mentioned—at the stable late Mr. Farringtons without the South Gate.'

The *Hampshire Telegraph* for 2 June 1828 describes one of the occasions when the beating of the bounds took place. 'On Friday the Mayor of Chichester (T. Mills, Esq.) attended by some members of the Corporation, the Sergeants and a posse of boys, according to ancient custom, perambulated the city bounds. The usual complement of sundry buckets of water, and two or three cold baths in the river Lavant, formed the principal features of the occasion, which ended with a sumptuous dinner at the *Swan Inn*'.

Chapter Twelve

Whose Responsibility?

I T IS TIME NOW TO TAKE A CLOSER LOOK at the role of the City Council with regard to the Lavant; in particular the parts played by that authority and the river in the matter of the health of Chichester's inhabitants.

The attitude of the City Council as to its rights and responsibilities over the river Lavant was somewhat curious. For most of the 19th century it was quite happy to receive income from the leases of riparian properties; and was prepared— if not exactly happy—to undertake the necessary cleaning and repairing of the watercourse. But from time to time, some corporate doubts were raised on the subject. For instance, in September 1843, there was a motion before the Council that the Town Clerk be instructed to ascertain the right of the Corporation to the course of the Lavant where it was bounded by the properties of other parties. As the motion failed by three votes to six, nothing was done at the time. Eight years later, a committee was appointed 'to enquire into the ownership of the Lavant course and the rights and liabilities of the Council with reference thereto'. The committee reported that they doubted whether they could add any information to what was already known, in the absence of any documentary evidence. Reference was made to the granting of leases; for instance, in 1819 to Mr. Figgis for a portion of the Lavant Course adjoining Snag Lane, and in 1839 to Mr. Gatehouse for a section at South Gate. (A century earlier, Mr. John Atwood had paid £15 and 12 bottles of wine for a 40 year lease of buildings on the Lavant Bridge.)

The committee submitted that any rights over the course held by the Corporation must have accrued to them either as owners of adjoining lands, or as Lords or Quasi Lords of the Manor, and as such they were entitled to a territorial interest in the course. However, if the Corporation had any rights as owners of adjacent lands, these rights must be limited to the parts of the course adjoining those lands. In any case, they should be limited to the ancient boundaries of the city, and not affected by any extension under more recent municipal acts.

As the Corporation had already taken on the burthen (*sic*) of cleaning and repairing the bed of the river, the committee went on, it was now too late to dispute such responsibilities. They did not consider that the Corporation could legally be called upon to repair the roads or approaches to the Lavant, though admitting that it had shared the cost of repairing the Duke of Richmond's section near the South Gate some years earlier.

The question of rights and liabilities continued to crop up from time to time. As late as 1886 the Council was once again considering its liability to expend money on the Lavant Course beyond the city limits (and incidentally to enquire into the cause of pollution of the stream). By eight votes to six, it was agreed to ask the Town Clerk by what authority the Council was justified in such expenditure. The response was not very helpful; so far as the Town Clerk knew it was the practice of the Corporation to do so, and he believed there was evidence of such custom over the past 40 years.

Our story would gain little by a recital of the various leases. One will suffice, memorable if only for the name of the lessee, Sir Fortunatus Dwarrus. The conditions of this lease, of March 1840, were typical of many, being subject to 'a power of the Council to widen and deepen the portions of the Lavant Course which belong to or adjoin such properties, and to widen and heighten the arches over the same if they shall think fit'.

For much of the 19th century there is detailed information as to the cost of repairing and maintaining the Lavant Course, but as the work of the City Council gets more complex references in the minutes get fewer, until they are finally absorbed in general expenditure. During the 40 years from 1837, about £1,500 was spent on this work, varying widely from year to year; from 3s. in 1844 to a total of £406 7s. 5d. in 1867 when the Lavant was becoming more and more of a problem. Early records even name the workmen: William Budden, Charles Peters, James Oakley. One wonders why, in 1840, an (unnamed) man 'usually employed to clean out the Lavant Course' should cease to be employed. Perhaps he was the same Mr. Budden to whom the Town Clerk was instructed to write in September 1843 directing him not to interfere in the cleansing of the Lavant Course.

One reads of repairs to a wheelbarrow, the sharpening of tools, the cost of carting timber, the supply of bricks. Some tradesmen's names are still familiar: Cover, Halsted, Lillywhite. There are references to the making of 'bunny drains'— defined in a Sussex dialect dictionary as wooden or brick drains laid under a road or gateway to carry off the water. In January 1890, following complaints from councillors about the state of the river bed, the City Surveyor replied, 'I can truthfully say that I have been at all times most painstaking that the Course should be kept clear, and I am constantly instructing the Corporation workmen ... Over £100 has been spent on the course during the past three years—not a small sum for keeping clear a narrow water course under three miles in length.' He went on in justification, 'All foreign matter is removed, principally tinware, leaves, branches, etc., leaving the water as far as possible to do the rest, a far more effective method than employing any amount of manual labour. When I caused an accumulation of leaves and twigs to be removed in an open waggon in day time some objection was made. [This was probably due to the unpleasant smell.] I submit, to have done this at night would have been useless, an unnecessary expense.' On receiving his report, the Council instructed the Surveyor to cleanse the course annually in the autumn in future.

Earlier, the Council was briefly at odds with a Mr. Johnson, who had contracted to carry out certain works on the Lavant. The contract was agreed in August 1857, to be proceeded with 'forthwith'. In the following July, he was told to carry out the work in accordance with the specifications, but a month later Alderman Wright reported that Mr. Johnson now stated positively that he would not perform the work in accordance with his contract. There followed a letter from the Town Clerk calling on him to complete his contract; failing which counsel would be taken and if necessary legal proceedings would follow. It would be interesting to know just what passed between the parties, but in February 1859 the Nuisances Removal Committee told the full Council that they did not think the Council would be interested in the discussions that had taken place or their reasons for recommending a compromise, but the upshot was that Mr. Johnson received a net sum of £179 0s. 7d.; being the contract amount plus additional work and less deductions for work not done and a reduced claim for disputed additional work.

22   The last of the Lavant, with the footpath from Fishbourne to Dell Quay.

Chapter Thirteen

A Carrier of Disease

A S CONCERN GREW OVER THE STATE OF THE LAVANT with its repeated flooding and baleful effect on public health, so the Council caused surveys to be made in attempts to relieve the situation: 1822, 1832, 1838, 1840, 1856, 1867 (two), 1872 and 1879. Some reports merely recommended limited alterations to the levels of the bed of the river, and sometimes this work was carried out. Others were more critical of the Council's attitude to the whole problem of sewage disposal and water supply. When this happened, the Council countered by calling in another surveyor of their choosing who would produce a more favourable report. Expressions of public concern over the state of the Lavant and its effect on local health were not lacking. In September 1852, the Guardians of the Poor wrote to the Corporation about numerous complaints in various parts of the City; and beg to call the earnest attention of the Town Council to a serious nuisance over which it has no control, viz. the Lavant Course which is now in many places in a most filthy and disgusting Condition and highly prejudicial to the Health of the Inhabitants in the Neighbourhood of the Course.' The Town Clerk was instructed to write such answer as should be approved by the Mayor.

Two years later, the Council's reaction to a recent Act of Parliament relating to Sanitary Measures and Duties and Powers of Local Authorities was to pass on its responsibilities to the local population. It issued an Address to Citizens recommending them to remove filth from their premises and to take pains to provide ample supplies of wholesome water. Just how they were to do this in the circumstances was not explained. The Address cannot have had much effect. In July 1856 the Nuisances Removal Committee was reporting that 'The Lavant Course is well known to be the Receptacle of numerous Bodies of Filth. For the whole extent of its Course through the City it is used for the reception of the Privy Soil of almost all the adjacent Houses. The Sanitary Inspector has served notices to Owners or Occupiers to discontinue the practice.'

One of the Lavant's industrial uses was in connection with the tannery in Westgate. The earliest reference to the tanyard itself is in a recital of a deed of 1703, although the records of St Bartholomew Parish for 1624/5 contain an inventory of a tanner. During the first half of the 18th century it was owned by knackers and fellmongers rather than full-time tanners. It expanded from 1796. The master's house still stands, owned by the County Council. In 1851, 18 labourers were employed, six of them living in the adjoining row of cottages, owned by the Shippam family. William Hoare's Jubilee reminiscences mention the tanyard, as having been at one time very open to the view of passers-by, 'which was not very pleasant at times, but within the last few years the Lavant course had been arched over. That and the premises at the Tanyard have been much improved by Messrs. Gibbings Harrison, which has made a very pleasant entrance to the town.' The last days of the business are described in Bernard Price's book, *Sussex: People, Places, Things.*

In November 1856, the Council received a letter written on behalf of Mr. George Henty (himself a councillor) at the Brewery, and Mr. William Norman at the Tannery, threatening legal proceedings against the Council as the legal authority for the removal of nuisances. But by August 1875 relations between the two businesses were less cordial. The Medical Officer of Health reported on the very offensive state of the Lavant at South Gate and West Gate. Mr. David Henty had made a serious charge against Mr. Gibbings, the new owner of the tanyard. It was found that a number of horns had accumulated and the course below was in a very foul state, 'to which it appears to me [commented the officer] Messrs. Henty contributed their full proportion'. Henty had threatened to summon the M.O.H. to give evidence, 'but', said the doctor, 'I doubt if it will answer his purpose to do so'.

Chichester's notoriety was spreading. Whereas Alexander Hay, the Sussex historian, could write in 1804 that the city enjoyed the advantage of most excellent water, by 1866 a London newspaper was describing the place as 'Preeminent for its beastliness'. The Rev. Charles Anthony Swainson, Prebendary of Firle from 1856 to 1887, expressed the feelings of many: 'We must have good water. The cry is heard in many quarters and must be attended to ... People die from water that is declared to be pure and bright and wholesome but which the simplest test shews to be poisonous if not stinking.' He quoted a local councillor as saying, 'I don't believe that bad water is the cause of fever. My water is good and I have never been ill.'

As public concern continued so, increasingly, did government interference, as it was looked upon by the city councillors. Twenty-eight inhabitants of South Gate petitioned about the state of the sewerage there, particularly about the uncovered Lavant. A London specialist, Dr. Lawson, recorded in 1866 that the Lavant was the main sewer for the city. He estimated that the cost of a proper sewage scheme would be £12,500 and a further £15,000 for a water supply scheme. In September of that year, a letter was received from the Local Government Act Office calling attention to conditions in the city and virtually threatening to appoint persons to carry out the appropriate regulations if action was not taken. It stated that there had been 12 deaths from cholera in the past few weeks; so the Council spent £11 3s. 6d. on cleaning the Lavant Course.

A house-to-house inspection of 1,739 properties revealed the following situation:

No. of houses with sickness	34
Dirty houses	43
Unfit for habitation	1
Privies emptying into Lavant	6
Full cesspools	39
Full privies	97
Houses with bad water	75
Complaints re Lavant Course	10
Houses keeping pigs	66
No. of pigs kept	251

The population at this time was 8,075.

At this period, several courts existed between St Pancras and the Lavant. Typical was St Pancras Place, described as a court with four houses, partly unoccupied. 'The whole court is foul and the stench intolerable.' It was decided to serve a notice on the owner, a Mr. Clark who, living at Charity Farm, Fareham, was far enough away not to notice the stench. The Council's general reaction was, once again, to call for an alternative opinion on water supply and sewage, but by January 1867 Mr. Arnold Taylor of the Local Government Act Office in London had added his word on 'The Scandalous Situation', as he called it. Little is spared, either to the Council of the time or the present-day researcher studying the City minutes. He noted that until recently it had been the practice for privies to be built over the bed of the stream, though they were now to have independent pits. When the Lavant was running, people used to pull a brick or two out of the back wall so that the Lavant might scour out their contents. He went on: 'Wherever the Lavant is accessible by eye or nose it was in a most offensive condition.'

It was ordered that Mr. Taylor's report should be printed and circulated, but by October 1867 the Council had managed to obtain a report from a Mr. Hawkesley refuting some of the mortality statistics and Mr. Taylor's comments on the insanitary conditions. This may have appeased the City Council, but not central government. In April 1869 the Home Secretary wrote, asking what had been done in response to Mr. Taylor's report. The Nuisances Committee considered this letter 'most ungracious and uncalled for', and felt there was no foundation in fact for the charges that the sanitary condition of Chichester was entirely bad, or that the death rate was unduly high, or that there was an absence of proper drainage! The same committee felt able to report only two months later that there was no existing nuisance in the city.

Nevertheless by September 1869 came a solicitor's letter from the central authority with the Government's threat of stringent measures to compel the drainage of Chichester and the creation of a proper water supply. This was followed by a questionnaire with 55 headings from the Sanitary Commissioners. Question No.27: 'If you have had any special outbreaks of disease since 1853, explain the nature of the disease and give the dates.' Answer: 'There have been no such special outbreaks since 1853.' No.28: 'Are there any districts specially affected by fever, diarrhoea, consumption or cholera?' Answer: 'No.' These were the Council's official replies, despite the fact that in 1866 no less than twelve deaths from cholera had occurred in the St Pancras area of the city, and again the Nuisances Removal Committee reported that the city continues in the usual healthy state in its sanitary condition.

PLAN OF CHICHESTER.

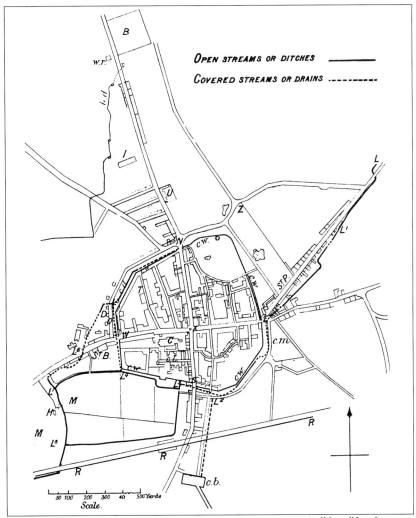

OPEN STREAMS OR DITCHES ——————

COVERED STREAMS OR DRAINS ----------

50 100 200 300 40 500 Yards
Scale.

DANGERFIELD.LITH.22.BEDFORD ST. COVENT GARDEN.

B Barracks
C Cathedral
D Dairy, in Orchard Street
E Eastgate
H Milking hovel
I Infirmary
L Lavant Stream
L¹ Houses with enteric fever in 4ᵗʰ quarter of 1878.
L² Inlet of flood relief pipe.
L³ Stream branches: modern cut (N°1.) goes south.

L⁴ Stream branches again: modern cut (N°2.) goes west.
L⁴toW Stream in Culvert under ⌐ Dʳ Tyacke's garden.
WtoL⁵ Stream in Culvert under ⌐ Orchard Street.
L⁶ Stream in Culvert returning under Westgate.
L⁷ Junction with cut (N°2.)
L⁸ Junction with cut (N°1.
M Meadows.
N Northgate.
c.l. Canon Lane
c.m Cattle Market

O Orchard Street.
S.ᵗP.St. Pancras.
R Railway.
S Southgate.
T Tower Street.
U Union Workhouse.
W Westgate
X Market Cross.
Z Depôt of City Refuse.
b.d. Barracks drainage (overflow)
c.b. Canal basin
c.d. "Campus" ditch.
c.w.City Walls.
w.r. Water reservoir.

23 Typhoid Map, 1879.

Chapter Fourteen

A Clean Bill of Health at Last

SO THINGS CONTINUED FROM YEAR TO YEAR. The Westhampnett Union Board of Guardians complained about the state of the Lavant at Appledram Common. The councillors' complacency continued. They felt that, considering the extraordinary wet season, there had been no prevalence of disease of any kind to assume that Chichester's health was any worse than other places in the Kingdom, although they must have been less than happy about the true state of affairs. Much was wrong back at St Pancras. There was effluent from Mr. Cutten's coach works; complaints about Mrs. Budden's property, about Budden's Court and Farr's Court, east of the *Plough and Harrow*. As for Mr. Henty's pub, the *Coach and Horses*, the Medical Officer of Health found a cart load of very offensive whelks, making matters tenfold worse by stench and obstruction. By 1879, Budden's Court was the worst place left in Chichester, being absolutely unfit for human habitation. And Mrs. Osborne's habits were inconceivably dirty (though we are spared the details!). Dr. Freeland, the Medical Officer of Health, was still giving warning that in future the debris and rubbish from the Lavant Course should not be turned over upon the banks adjoining houses, which exposed large foul surfaces to swelter and putrefy, but should be carefully carried away.

Soon a fresh menace was added to the health hazards of the poor, long-suffering citizens of Chichester. Poor is the word, since it was of course in the worst slum areas that disease was most prevalent. In March 1879, the Local Government Board was making enquiries into what the Council called an 'alleged' typhoid outbreak, and had sent down its own specialist, Dr. Hubert Airey. He was a man after the M.O.H.'s own heart, for Dr. Frederick John Freeland, 'Surgeon, Apothecary, legally qualified Medical Practitioner', had for years been vainly trying to make the Council understand and accept the seriousness of the unhealthy state of the city. One senses that his patience had come to an end when in July 1879 he tells the councillors: 'The medical men of this city seem agreed on one point, that is, pollution of the Lavant is a source of serious danger. To my knowledge the water has been used to wash milk pails; worse still, for drink for children ... After what has happened under my own observations in one place and upon several occasions, I feel bound to give a warning which under any circumstances it might have been prudent to accept, my responsibility having been exhausted in offering it, I could have no desire to express opinions based upon long experience, upon unwilling ears.' He then reminds the Council once more of the frequency of infectious fever along the course of the river, before setting out yet again his own position and his powers as Medical Officer of Health.

Dr. Airey's report, presented in September, was a vindication of all that Freeland had maintained for so long. 'I suspected a particular dairy in Orchard Street as being the vehicle of typhoid infection. The Dairy's water is drawn from a well under the same roof. The well is situated in a sharp bend of the Watercourse underlying Orchard Street [Potter's dairy?] and it is conceivable that it might derive impure admixture from the watercourse. Five cows are pastured on the meadow in either side of the Lavant which when flowing (for it is dry in summer and autumn) washed the east, south and west outskirts of the city, receiving in its course large quantities of filth, and finally makes its way to the sea. The cows no doubt drink of the water when flowing. At other times from a spring in the meadow. That the Lavant at the end of January and the beginning of February was carrying typhoid excreta there can, I think, be little room for doubt ... The privies stand on either side of the stream, most of them at the very edge, those across the stream being accessible by a plank bridge. The insecure brickwork of the privy pit allows excremental matter to ooze visibly into the bed of the stream. Wells in the back yard yield such bad water that one of the inhabitants confessed to using the water of the Lavant in preference. Slops were frequently poured into the Lavant Course. Among these cottages there was a good deal of typhoid in 1878, extending to January of this year ...' Dr. Airey then described in detail the course of the Lavant, not forgetting the brewery and tannery adding largely to the pollution. He reported that some privies had not been emptied for the past eight years. The only favourable comment he was able to make was a reference to the supply of clean water that had existed for the past four years, being supplied by a private company from a strong spring at the head of the Fishbourne Creek, carried to a reservoir on the west side of the Broyle Road (w.r. in the diagram).

It was perhaps typical of the Council of the time that the report was not considered until the following November, and even then without reference to a proper drainage scheme. The following September, the Medical Officer of Health was still reporting that the streets 'were more stenchy than I ever knew them to be'. A young man from St Pancras died from typhoid in April 1881, with three more deaths in 1885. Another cause of trouble was the insanitary condition of the ditch carrying sewage from the Infirmary to the Campus at the north end of Orchard Street. One feels that with all his responsibilities and lack of support Dr. Freeland was fully earning his £100 per annum. As he said 18 months later, 'Everyone will admit that improvement is desirable, but the exact method may have to be determined'.

Still the Council moved at its customary pace. In January 1889 a special committee was appointed to visit other towns and report on the best system of drainage. At the same time, the Corporation offered £40,000 to buy out the local water company, but they were not interested. In September the Committee presented its report, confirming to the Council what many outsiders had known for some time. They found that most towns had already been drained, with improvement to public health. Chichester was behind the times and was still as unhealthy as in 1865. Despite the absence of noxious trades or factories the death rate was 22.7 per 1,000. They recommended acceptance of a scheme costing £15,435 submitted by Mr. Charles Jones, a past President of the Association of Municipal Engineers and Surveyors. Typically the Council deferred consideration until the following November and typically again did not consider it then. At that meeting, however, Dr. Freeland resigned from his post as M.O.H. The reason given was ill health, but one cannot help feeling that disappoinment and frustration must have contributed to his decision. It comes as no surprise that, two months later, there were further attempts at delay for yet more examinations of the sanitary condition of the city. At that same meeting, Dr. Freeland's successor was appointed. Mr. J.M. Percival, Surgeon and Apothecary, must have been an officer more to the taste of at least some of the councillors. In his first report, in February 1890, he wrote: 'The recent statement by one in authority of sixty four cases of typhoid fever in the city in the last eighteen months is, I consider, most misleading and calculated to give a false and most unjust idea of the sanitary conditions, and greatly to the disadvantage in every way. Chichester in the past twelve months at least has been a healthy place and in a good sanitary state'.

Despite this reassuring opinion, the Council decided to set up another Special Committee, to prepare a scheme of main drainage, and report back. A new scheme, drawn up by Sir Frederick Bramwell, was submitted to the Council within six months, in October 1890. Despite further attempts to delay matters, Bramwell was formally appointed Engineer in charge. The diehards were still at it in January 1891, in an attempt to limit his expenses for the completion of plans and estimates to £100. His actual fee when settled was £250. In March the new Medical Officer of Health was reporting that out of 675 waters examined, 135 were utterly bad and 144 others showed signs of impurity. Nevertheless he could still say 'I cannot say that I anticipate any very marked improvement in the death rate in consequence of drainage'. By June the plans were approved and the estimate of £21,000 accepted. Meanwhile the Water Company had declined to enter into negotiations with the Corporation on the lines proposed, that is, for an independent valuation to be made of the undertaking.

But despite all the references back, all the tactics of procrastination, matters did move slowly forward. Mr. Marshall Hall was retained on behalf of the Council at the inevitable public inquiry. A resident engineer, Mr. Baldwin Latham, was appointed to oversee the sewage works construction and negotiate with owners of affected properties. So that at last, in February 1897, the year of celebration of Victoria's sixty glorious years, the engineer was able to issue his Final Report and Certificate, and on 11 June the Town Clerk announced that the Chichester Corporation Water Bill had received the Royal Assent.

Chichester now had a proper drainage system and owned its own water undertaking; which seems an appropriate point at which to close this sordid chapter in the career of our river.

24   Westgate Fields.

25   The Lavant in the grounds of the College of Further Education.

Chapter Fifteen

On to Appledram

WE CAN NOW TAKE UP THE MAIN THREAD OF OUR STORY, with the Lavant no longer running alongside Westgate as it did in William Hoare's time, but still skirting the former tannery building, now satisfactorily converted into offices for the County Council. From here it runs partly through waste land, then across the playing fields of the College of Technology, to pass under the Chichester-Portsmouth railway line. Further culverting of the stream took place during the Second World War, in 1940 and again in 1944. In May 1940, the Southern Railway requested the Sussex River Catchment Board to close the sluice at Southgate for about two months so that the work could be carried out. The Board had earlier reported to the Ministry of Transport that the Lavant had a tendency to flood across the meadows on the north side of the railway, and to flood the approach to the footbridge. This bridge carries the public footpath from the College to Appledram Lane, roughly following the line of the river. In March 1944, there was further correspondence between the authorities and the Ministry of War Transport concerning the provision of additional sidings on the down side of Chichester station. This work, under Defence Regulation no.50, was presumably in preparation for D-Day operations, being described as work of national importance and of extreme urgency.

The river itself can be seen at two points along Terminus Road, one being the rubbish-laden section which is a continuation of the Southgate overflow, the other the main stream, again a rather pathetic sight at this point. Conditions improve as we pick up the line again to the south of the Chichester By-pass and follow the stream by stile and footpath across fields and Appledram Lane, where it passes to the south of the sewage works and—at last—makes its way to the sea via the Fishbourne channel and Chichester Harbour.

Historically, however, this is not the end of its adventures. As we have seen, our little river has over the years been subjected to innumerable man-made changes. Many of them were minor, but from time to time the proposal has been put forward that the Lavant should revert to its original line in order to avoid altogether its passage round the city. As Charles Dixon, Engineer to the Council, wrote in his report in September 1856: 'Of course, nothing but diverting the Course before it enters the Town would secure it against *all* floods.' Again, as recently as 1958, the West Sussex River Board's annual report contained an item for future works, subject to Government approval on capital expenditure, for the diversion of the Lavant around the city, at a cost of £120,000. This item disappeared from later reports.

The most ambitious of the schemes which never came to fruition comes from a much earlier period. As Adolphus Ballard, Mayor of Chichester in Diamond Jubilee year, wrote in his history of the city published in 1898: 'In 1585 the citizens

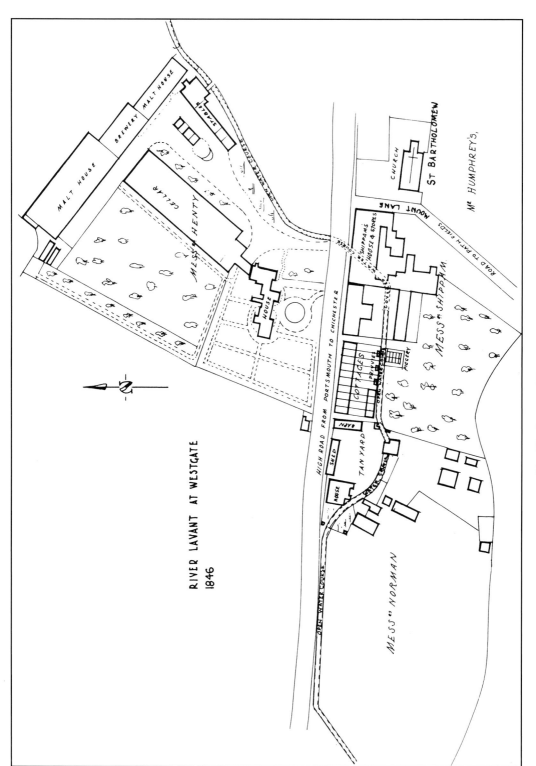

26 The Lavant at Westgate, 1846.

27   The Lavant near Appledram Lane.

again took action for the improvement of their harbour; they represented to Parliament that Dell Quay was a mile and a half from the city, and that by reason of the deepness and foulness of the ways, the cost of carriage from the Quay to the city was very expensive. Moreover as there was no room for both warehouses or lodgings at the Quay, it was very inconvenient both for the storage of goods and for the accommodation of seamen and merchants. They therefore obtained an Act of Parliament for bringing the Lavant by a new cut channel to the suburbs of the city. The cut was to start at Dell Quay and Fishbourne, and as the citizens were empowered to utilise all brooks and streams of water near the cut, it seems as though they meant to deepen the bed of the Lavant and so bring vessels to the West Gate of the city.' William Camden's *Britannia* (1610) refers to the proposal: 'The haven is badde and somewhat farre off, and in that regard not so commodious: which nevertheless the cittizens goe now in hand to make more convenient by digging of a new channel.' The proposed channel was to have been two hundred feet wide, but nothing came of this grandiose scheme, and Chichester had to wait two hundred years for its canal.

Even at the end of its journey, our stream was still in trouble. In January 1871, the Town Clerk was instructed to write to a Mr. Stanford pointing out the effect of an obstruction created by him at the outfall of the water at Appledram, and requesting that it should be removed. And in his report in 1877, the Medical Officer of Health refers to a fresh cutting having been made at Appledram Common, and the deepening of the river bed in the Rymans, thus draining the surrounding fields but still acting as a catchpit for filth from West Gate (how difficult it is to escape

28 Plan: Diversion at Harbour sluice, 1945.

from it) and influencing the character of the outflow upon the marshes and the deposit left on subsidence of the water. Richard Ratcliff, in his *History of Apuldram* published in 1986, writes of flooding in the area, where one of the most vulnerable points was the estuary of the Lavant on the borders between Fishbourne and Appledram, though this was later protected by sea walls and sluices. He also mentions a tidal mill, operated by water coming up the mouth of the Lavant, on the Fishbourne boundary at the north-east corner of the common. In this area of the harbour, too, there flourished another local industry, the panning of salt, until the imported product made this no longer an economic proposition. F.H. Arnold, writing in 1866, says that these salt works were formerly of as great reputation as any in the country.

In June 1943, Chichester's Town Clerk wrote to the River Catchment Board (there have been so many changes in the responsible authority over the years) to say that the outfall sluice adjoining the sewage disposal works at Appledram was in a dangerous state, and asking for repairs to be carried out without delay. In the same month, the County Surveyor concurred in the need for repairs. A mere 12 months later, the Board also agreed that it was in a bad state. Their solution was that, instead of carrying out repairs, it would be simpler to cut a new course for the river and to fill in the old bed. They stated that this section of the river was technically held by the Ecclesiastical Commissioners, so perhaps an exchange of lands could be effected. That body, acting on the advice of their solicitors, agreed to make a free grant of the land—about one rood—subject to their costs being paid. All seemed to be going well: the Ministry of Agriculture and Fisheries, on 2 September 1944, approved the estimated cost of £1,250, agreeing to pay 60 per cent, with the rest coming from the Catchment Board.

But nothing is simple. In the November, the Ecclesiastical Commissioners discovered that the land involved actually formed part of the Winchester Bishopric Permanent Estates, and moreover 'a bishop has no powers under the Ecclesiastical Licensing Acts to make a free grant of land'. So a nominal consideration of £5 was suggested and accepted, all costs to be paid by the grantees, who after much discussion turned out to be the Mayor, Aldermen and Citizens of Chichester. Two years after the original request for urgent repairs, the conveyance was signed, with one intriguing clause, that the Bishopric reserved to itself 'all coal and mines of coal (if any) and other minerals'. However unlikely that prospect, the idea of a pit shaft or an oil rig on that one rood of land is hardly to be contemplated!

There is a nice tailpiece to the above story. The contract for carrying out the necessary work was given to Messrs. G.A. Neal and Sons. They admitted having no previous experience of this class of work, although they had done drainage and road works. The firm needed faggots for the job which were to be obtained from a depot at Sidlesham Ferry, but when their men went there to collect them, they were just in time to see a military type lorry in the process of removing the precious faggots. They cost £6 per hundred, and it was impossible at that time of year to find fresh supplies, even if the labour had been available. Fifty were later found at a Royal Air Force Regiment Camp, where they were being used for firewood. A sergeant on the site promised to make enquiries—which not surprisingly is the last we hear about them.

Chapter Sixteen

'Rippling Waves ...'

29   The Last of the Lavant.

SO WE COME TO THE END OF OUR STORY, as the waters of the Lavant merge with the tides of Chichester Harbour. As I write, the river is once again making its annual appearance. Long may it continue to do so, to give pleasure to people on its way from the Downs to the sea.

I give the last word to our local poet, Charles Crocker, with the final verse of his poem on that much troubled, much loved river.

> Soft as the dew the deepening shades descend
> And spread a solemn, sacred calm around,
> Till night's broad wings o'er all the scene extend,
> Naught breaks the stillness save the gentle sound
> Of rippling waves, that glimmer as they bound
> On their dark way. Who would not wish to dwell
> For ever where such tranquil joys are found?
> But Duty speaks in yonder curfew bell,
> And warns me to depart—blest scenes, awhile farewell.

Chapter Sixteen

The Floods of January 1994
A Pictorial Record

30   Floodwater at Westhampnett.

31   Chichester by-pass between Whyke and Bognor roundabouts.

32   The flooded A27 east of Chichester.

33   The A27 and Maudlin Farm from the air.

34 Bailey bridge on the A259 at Merston.

35   Bailey bridge and pontoon at Westhampnett roundabout.

36   Sandbags at the Castle Market, Chichester.

37   West Sussex Fire Brigade's sandbags.

38   The River Lavant in full flow through Chichester.

39   The Hornet, looking towards Eastgate Square.

40   Floodwater in the Hornet, looking west.

41 Floodwater in the Hornet, looking east.

42   Preparations in East Street, Chichester.

43   Milk float in Yapton.

Chapter Seventeen

The Floods of November 2000

44 Rising water in Delling Lane, Bosham.

45 Flooding: St Pancras, Chichester.

46   New Park Road, Chichester.

47   Flood relief piping at Old Market Avenue, Chichester.

Source Materials

Ballard, Adolphus, *History of Chichester*
Chichester City Council Minute Books
Chichester Society Newsletter
Cunliffe, Barry, *The Regni*
Curwen, E.C., *The Archaeology of Sussex*
Gentleman's Magazine, 1792
Goodwood Archives
Hay, Alexander, *History of Chichester*
Hoare, William, *An Account of Conversations between Old Age and William Young*
Keating, Leslie, *The Book of Chichester*
Kelly's Directories of Sussex
Lavant Parish Magazines
Price, Bernard, *Changing Chichester*
Price, Bernard, *Sussex: People, Places, Things*
Ratcliff, Richard, *History of Apuldram*
Serraillier, Ian, *All Change at Singleton*
Simon, Noel, *The Edward James Foundation*
Singleton, West Dean, East Dean Church Guide
Spershott, James, *Memoirs*
Swainson, C.A., *A Few Words To Those Who Have The Welfare of Chichester At Heart*
Southern Water Authority and predecessors, Annual Reports
Sussex Archaeological Collections
Sussex Record Society, vol.62
Victoria County History of Sussex
West Sussex County Record Office, Miscellaneous Papers
West Sussex Land Drainage Records
Wright, Tom, *The Gardens of Britain*, vol.4

Index

Airey, Dr. Hubert, 43, 44
Appledram, 43, 47, 49, 51
Atwood, John, 36

Basin Road, 30
Beating the Bounds, 34, 35
Bennett, Fred, 7
Bishop Otter College, 13
Bramwell, Sir Frederick, 45
Breweries, 23, 34, 44
Bridge Road, 24

Canal, 49
Charlton, 4, 9
Chichester City Council, 22, 23, 26, 30,
    36, 37, 38, 39, 40, 41, 43, 44, 45, 49, 51
Chichester Harbour, 1, 47
Chilgrove, 9
Cholera, 40, 41
City boundaries, 35
College Lane, 13, 14
Conduit Mead, 18
Crocker, Charles, 1, 2, 52
Cucumber Farm, 5

Dell Quay, 49
Drownings, 1, 11, 19, 20
Dwarrus, Sir Fortunatus, 37

East Dean, 1, 4,
East Lavant, 1, 9, 11, 12
Eastgate, 24, 26, 31
Edge, Rev. Peter, 21

Figgis, Mr., 36
Fishbourne Channel, 1, 47
Flooding, 1, 9, 11, 20, 24, 25, 26, 47
Florance, 23
Fordwater, 13, 19

Franklin Place, 26
Freeland, Dr. Frederick John, 43, 45

Gatehouse, George, 31, 36
Graylingwell, 14, 15
Green Lane, 24

Habin, Edward, 23, 26
Henty, David, 40, 43
Henty, George, 35, 40
Hoare, William, 30, 34, 39, 47
Horn, Daphne, 11
Hornet, The, 24

Infirmary, 44

Jacques, Charles, 23, 25
Jekyll, Gertrude, 8

Kenwood, William, 31
Kingsham, 25, 27

Lambourne, Mrs. G.N., 11
Latham, Baldwin, 45
Lavant, derivation of name, 1
Lavant, river, Poems, 1, 9, 52
Lavant, river, Prehistoric course, 3
Lavant, river, Source, 3, 4
Lavant, School, 9, 11
Legge, Rev. Henry, 10
Leprosy, 21

Market Avenue, 31
Mid Lavant, 1, 10
Millfield Close, 18
Mills: Chichester, 2, 18; Lavant, 2, 10;
    Westhampnett, 2, 15, 18

Needlemakers, The, 24

New Park Road, 24
Norman, William, 40

Orchard Street, 34, 35, 44
Oving Road, 24

Pagham Harbour, 19
Percival, J.M., 45
Potters Field, 34
Preston Farm, 9
Price, Bernard, 11, 40
Public Health, 36-45

Ratcliff, Rev. Richard, 51
Richmond, Dukes of, 9, 10, 15, 18, 22, 30

Sadler Family, 15, 18
St James's Hospital, 21, 22
St James's Post, 22, 35
St Pancras, 20, 22, 23, 24, 25, 41, 43, 44
Sanden, Dr. Thomas, 23
Serraillier, Ian, 4, 5
Sewage scheme, 44, 45
Sheep washing, 5, 11
Singleton, 1, 5, 13
Snag Lane, 25, 27, 30, 36
Southgate, 31, 33
Spershott, James, 22, 23, 24, 26
Spitalfield Lane, 22
Squitry Bridge, 34

Squitry Lane, 34
Story, Bishop, 21
Swainson, Rev. Charles, 40
Swanfield Drive, 22

Tannery, 34, 35, 39, 40, 47
Terminus Road, 47
Tozer Way, 24
Tucker, Trudy, 9, 11
Typhoid, 43, 44, 45

Walker, Rev. William, 22
War measures, 15, 47
Water authorities, 4, 10, 15, 19, 20, 33, 47, 51
Water meadows, 7, 9, 33
Water Plat, 18
Water supply, 9, 10, 40, 41, 44, 45
Watery Lane, 27
West Dean, 3, 7, 8
West Sussex County Council, 13, 19
Westgate, 1, 33, 49
Westhampnett, 15, 18
Westhampnett Road, 1, 19, 20, 22
Winchester Bishopric, 51
Winterbourne Road, 13
Women's Institute, 4
Wright, Tom, 8

Young, Rev. Arthur, 7